In May 1588, one of the [...] had ever seen set out fro[...] England — the 'invincib[...] [...]enty five heavily-armed galleons, twenty-five store ships and thirty smaller vessels.

It was an ill-fated fleet, and after losses in the English Channel a decision was taken to return to Spain. The commanders were ordered to sail out into the Atlantic, thus avoiding the dangers of the Irish coast. Not all obeyed the order. Many sought shelter on the west coast of Ireland, which became the graveyard of twenty-four or more ships.

This is a grim and tragic story which fills in the details of those historic weeks in the autumn and winter of 1588 ...

T. P. KILFEATHER was born in Sligo on Ireland's north-west coast. The story of the Armada shipwrecks — three were lost off this coastline — always fascinated him, an interest which remained through his journalistic career. His book is the result of the research which sought the facts behind the legend.

T.P. KILFEATHER

Ireland
Graveyard of the
Spanish Armada

ANVIL BOOKS

Published 1988 by Anvil Books Limited
90 Lower Baggot Street, Dublin 2

First published 1967
Reprinted 1979

ISBN 0 900068 43 4

Printed in Great Britain by
Richard Clay, Bungay, Suffolk

CONTENTS

CHAPTER ONE

THE YELLOW SUNSET

THIS is a story of stark tragedy. It begins on the rugged north-west coast of Ireland on an evening in September 1588, when a sun of baleful yellow lit the last moments of the day, and in its light the Atlantic heaved and surged with pitiless restlessness. It was an evening when death was in the screaming of the wind.

This was the scene in which twenty-four, maybe twenty-six, ships of the Spanish Armada were wrecked and more than 5,000 men died in terrible fashion—one of the greatest sea disasters of history. It happened long, long ago, but the passing of time does not lessen the poignancy nor the savagery of it all. On this September evening the wind had bent with invisible fingers the few stunted trees that grew in the bogland wastes on the edge of the Atlantic. It had urged the waves of the ocean into even greater fury against sheer cliffs and rocky headlands. Spume and sea-wrack marked the edge of the sullen power of the storm. Silhouetted against the yellow streak of the brief sunset, and far out to sea, there appeared the slender pencils of ship-masts almost bare of all sail.

These were some of the proud ships of the Spanish Armada. Astern, and still out of sight, were many more —most of their crews destined to meet shipwreck, drowning, summary and brutal execution, and a few—small in number—who were to make their way back to Spain. Mercifully the men who sailed in these ill-fated ships could not foresee their destiny. Three of the vessels came closer to land so that those on board could see the detail of the coast.

Dominating the skyline they saw a level-topped mountain running westward until it dropped in a 1,500-foot cliff to the low ground on the fringe of the Atlantic. The sides of this mountain were scored with deep clefts running from summit to base. This was Benbulben on the coast of County Sligo. From the sloping ground at its base there jutted out a peninsula named Mullaghmore, the finger of land which forms the division of Sligo Bay and Donegal Bay. To the seamen in the three great ships this peninsula seemed to offer a haven on its lee side. They steered for it, and as the wind abated the anchors splashed into the water. One of these vessels was the *San Juan de Sicilia,* a ship of 800 tons, with twenty-six guns and a complement of 343 men. The second of the three may have been the *Lavia* of 728 tons, armed with twenty-five guns and a company of 274 men, but there is no certain proof that this was her name. The third ship, too, was crowded, but in the archives or the stories of the handful of survivors of her wreck no name is given. For four days they swung at their anchorage, repairing sail and caulking as many of the leaking seams as they could reach. Without small boats they could not land to refill their water-casks or to obtain fresh food. Without a knowledge of the waters in which they were anchored they could not drift closer to shore lest they should run on hidden reefs. Luckless and unfortunate Spaniards! If they had sailed ten miles southwards they would have reached the estuary of the River Garavogue. There, although Sligo was a garrison town, they would have found a less perilous anchorage. Twenty miles northwards there was the sheltered anchorage at Killybegs in Donegal Bay. The Spaniards could not have picked a more dangerous place on the entire coast to send down the few anchors they did possess. Even today there is a section of this coast so exposed to the fierce winds of the Atlantic that the storm-blast is called the 'Munninane hurricane'. The wind that sweeps across Munninane bog is, indeed, terrible in its strength with the pressure of 4,000 miles of ocean behind it.

This was the evening when the baleful yellow sunset

silhouetted the three great ships of the Armada in their lonely anchorage on a strange and unknown coast. That yellow sunset is still a warning to those who live on Ireland's north-west coast. More often than not it follows a storm of great strength, but more importantly it invariably foretells another storm. This new unleashing of the winds was not long in coming. Rain-curtains began to move from seaward at great speed. In their centre was a black mass, at their edges was a grey shroud, and, as they travelled, the water became white with the deluge. Then came the wind. At first it was a shrill whimper, then a howling shriek, and once more the inshore waters became a frenzied and tumultuous sea. In this wild and fierce wind sweeping over a darkened sea the Spaniards cast glances of fear towards their straining cables of hemp and prayed that they would hold. But they did not hold, and the hundreds of men in the *San Juan de Sicilia* and the two other ships were but hours away from eternity.

One by one the hempen cables parted. Reeling in the wave-troughs the three ships were cast on that rugged shore. Those on board heard the splintering crash as jagged rocks tore gaping holes in wooden hulls. One by one they heeled over and were pounded to small pieces of wreckage by the enormous weight and power of the curving waves. Hundreds of men were drowned within minutes. Those who did reach the shore alive were captured and slain by sword-stab of the Queen's men, and if they evaded capture they were beaten insensible and robbed of all their possessions, even to the clothes they wore, by the inhabitants of the district who crowded to the scene of the wrecks. A small band of not more than twenty staggered from the surf unseen. These were later helped to reach the castles of O'Rourke at Dromahaire, County Leitrim, and MacClancy at Rosclogher, on the shore of Lough Melvin, the lake which forms part of the boundaries of Leitrim and Donegal. The aftermath of these three wrecks was described by Geoffrey Fenton, industrious official of his masters in

London, in a report which he sent to Lord Burghley.

He wrote: 'I numbered in one strand of less than five miles in length above 1,000 corpses of men which the sea had driven upon the shore, and the country people told me the like was in other places.'

Lord Deputy Fitzwilliam added this account: 'After leaving Sligo town I journeyed towards Bundrowse and so to Ballyshannon. Riding along the seashore, I went to see the bay where some of these ships were wrecked and where, as I heard not long before, lay 1,200 or 1,300 of the dead bodies. I rode along that strand nearly two miles (but left behind me a long mile or more) and then turned off that shore—in both of which places they said that had seen it there lay a great store of timber of wrecked ships . . . more than would have built four of the greatest ships I ever saw, besides many great boats, cables and other cordage answerable thereto, and such masts for bigness and length as in my knowledge I never saw any two that could make the like.'

The strand was Streeda strand and the exact place of the shipwreck has been known ever since as 'Carrig na Spainneach', a rock-reef off the little island of Dernish, Ahamlish parish, the centre of which is the present-day village of Grange, County Sligo. Supporting this traditional pin-pointing of shipwreck is a map made in 1609 which has an inscription over the location: 'Three Spanish shipps here cast ashore, Anno Domini 1588.'

The fate of these three great ships was shared by others in the great fleet of Spain along the Irish coast. They were wrecked in three groups—in Munster; from Galway to Killala bay; and those wrecked in County Sligo and Ulster. The names of some of these ill-fated vessels are known. In other cases their names can be guessed at with a certain degree of accuracy.

The unfortunate men who sailed in them were certainly the most luckless of men. Those that survived shipwreck were in many cases hanged or put to the sword after their capture. Groups of them who surrendered in the hope of receiving mercy were set upon and butchered, others were hunted like wild animals and killed as soon as they were captured. One large band of survivors was kept in confinement for many days. All of these men were then brought from their prisons in small batches and slaughtered in a single day. Only in the North-West, where the Irish chieftains had retained some independence of English rule, did these hapless Spaniards receive shelter and hospitality. In Mayo, Galway, Clare and in Kerry, the Irish were so fearful of their English overlords that no aid was given to the exhausted seafarers. With an apparent sense of satisfaction an English official recorded: 'Spaniards drowned, 5,600; Spaniards slain and put to execution who escaped out of the ships that were lost, 1,100.'

The same chronicler told his masters in London: '. . . in the opinion of some of the best shipmasters of that great fleet which were taken prisoner and executed, it is not like that 20 ships of all the whole fleet should return to Spain. For besides those that were taken and that perished, both in the Narrow Seas and here upon the coast of Ireland, most of their ships had many leaks and wanted victual and fresh water, and were very sore rent, torn and battered in many places, and bulged underwater in suchwise as very few can hold out any long time.'

The estimate of the number of ships of the Spanish Armada that would make their way back to Spain was inaccurate, but the description of the sorry state of the ships and of their provisions was only too true.

Along Ireland's north-west and south-west coast are 'Spanish Rocks' or 'Spanish Points'. Near these locations are slight, grass-grown mounds that are called 'The Spaniards' Grave'. They are reminders of a great tragedy of the sea and memorials to man's inhumanity to man in an age when cruelty and callous indifference to suffering were a normal part of life.

CHAPTER TWO

FEAR WAS THE SPUR

THE IRELAND to which the men of the Spanish Armada sailed, in search of safe anchorages at which they could repair their battered vessels and replenish their stores of food and water, was an island ruled by men with fear in their hearts. Outnumbered by the Irish whom they held in subjection for Queen Elizabeth the First, they had heard that a great invasion-force from Spain had been reported in the English Channel. It was a time when weeks might elapse before news could reach Ireland from London. But of this they were certain; if a strong force of Spaniards were allowed to land in Ireland the life of an Englishman would not be worth a single groat. The Spanish ships were big and they bristled with heavy guns. Their decks were crowded with soldiers—and the soldiers of Spain were the finest in the Europe of those days. Should they come ashore and group their forces, Ireland would be in a blaze of insurrection. If that were to happen, those who served Queen Elizabeth in the midst of a sullen, half-conquered people would be very dead indeed. They had no barracks or fortresses to hold hundreds of prisoners. They had no means of feeding a large number of captives. They had so few men under arms that they could not afford large escorts to bring their prisoners to Dublin. These men who were imposing their will upon the Irish people responded with a will to the stern order to kill all Spaniards wherever they might be found. The Spanish soldiers and sailors had been paid their wages before the Armada sailed. Many of the Spanish noblemen were richly dressed with velvet coats and cloaks, and they wore gold chains and rings. It was to be expected that the sailors and the soldiers would land with a little bag of gold coins lashed to their wrists. It was to

>e expected, too, that the noblemen and the officers of
Spain would strive to save their jewellery, their gold and
silver table-plate.

To comply with the order to kill out of hand without
mercy would have been a discharge of duty for the English,
but it was also an order which would reward them with
much loot if it were carried promptly into effect. Yet it
would be wrong to assume that all the death and suffering
endured by the Spanish castaways were caused by men of
English birth and blood. From Dublin Castle to London
went a report that 'the Irish are greedy for spoil'. The
Irish—as they have always done—served in the armed
forces of England's kings and queens. And it was the Irish
who, in many instances, robbed the helpless castaways and
stripped them naked before handing them over to the
officials of Queen Elizabeth. It was an Irishman who
hanged all the Spanish captives who fell into his clutches
in County Clare, and it was an Irishman who directed the
massacre of a band of Spaniards whose ship was wrecked
on the coast of County Mayo.

That ship was the *Gran Grin*, a large merchant vessel of
,160 tons which was converted for naval warfare with an
armament of twenty-eight guns and provided with a complement of 329 sailors and soldiers. Their commander was
Don Pedro de Mendoza. For days this vessel had been
wallowing in the heavy seas off the north-west coast. To
those on board it was clear that unless they could reach
land all of them would drown. The vessel was leaking
badly. Although men worked in relays at the pumps and
baled water from her flooded holds with wooden buckets,
she settled lower and lower in the heavy seas.

As they drifted nearer to land they saw hills that were
windswept and desolate. They did not know it, but on their
beam was Clew Bay with the bulk of Clare Island at its
entrance. On the northern side of the bay the mountains
began, high hills alternating with bare moorlands and
bog-filled valleys. Over to the east was the massive dome

of Nephin, then across a deep depression rose Birreencorragh, and further west the wild Nephinbeg range running northwards from Claggan mountain to Slieve Car.

They saw the island of Achill, windswept and bare, with Slievemore soaring to 2,000 feet and Croaghaun rising almost as high, and then they must have gazed with fear at the cliffs of Meenaun. A hundred men in charge of Don Pedro landed from the sinking ship on Clare Island. The island is rugged, 1,700 acres of bog and mountain. Today there are 150 inhabitants where, a hundred years ago, there were ten times that number. The number of those who lived there in the time of the first Elizabeth is not known. It was then the stronghold of Granuaile (Grainne Ni Mhaille), the remains of whose castle is today a national monument. She was mistress of a large section of western territory and once visited the court of Elizabeth —where she astonished the courtiers by refusing a title on the ground that she could not accept an honour from an equal.

Two days after the commander of the *Gran Grin* and his companions had landed on the island, the ship continued to drift until it finally grounded at Toorglass on the Corraun peninsula. Sixteen men who had remained on board came ashore 'wearing chains of gold'. These men were made captive and were handed over to the Governor of Connacht by a tenant of the Earl of Ormond. On Clare Island the shipwrecked soldiers and sailors sought to leave in a mass escape by stealing the currachs of the islanders. These light, high-prowed craft probably meant the difference between survival and starvation to those who lived on Clare Island. But the plan was uncovered. On the orders of Dubhdara Rua O'Malley the Spaniards were attacked by the islanders, and all but two of them were killed in the fight—a Spaniard, and an Irishman from County Wexford who had sailed with the Armada. A few days later the Governor of Connacht was informed that 'at Clare Island a great ship with 700 men is clean sunk to the bottom.

One hundred were saved, but O'Malley killed all except one poor Spaniard and an Irishman of the County of Wexford. They brought a great quantity of treasure to the island.' The reputation of the O'Malleys was such that there is no record of the Queen's officers having made any effort to seize the treasure, whatever it may have been.

With some elation the Governor of Connacht passed the news to the Secretary of the Council, Geoffrey Fenton. In turn, Fenton sent a message with all speed to Lord Burghley in London. 'I hope,' he wrote, 'that it will raise a diffidence between the Spaniards and the Irish so long as the memory of the present transactions shall endure.' The advisers of Elizabeth were quick to see that if these stories of Irish atrocities upon the men who sailed in the Armada were to reach Spain, a wedge would be driven between two Catholic peoples. And these stories did reach Spain. The atrocity story is as old as warfare itself. The sad feature of the Clare Island massacre is that it was true. The English who used it for propaganda purposes had no reason to embellish it.

The attempted escape of the Spaniards from the island lends support to the theory that O'Malley desired to hold them captive until they could be handed over to the Queen's officials with whom he wished to curry favour. This is a theory which, no doubt, has enraged many of the clan O'Malley, but if Dubhdara Rua O'Malley had not been holding them against their will there would have been no need for the Spaniards to attempt to steal the islanders' currachs. It is probable that the Spaniards may have heard of another Armada ship which had anchored a few miles northwards of Clew Bay and had decided on making a break for freedom.

In faraway London the Duke of Ormond heard a rumour that among the castaways in Clew Bay was the leader of the Armada, the Duke of Medina Sidonia. He at once sent instructions that the Spanish leader was not to be placed in chains and that he was to have at his disposal the Duke

of Ormond's horse. The rumour, of course, was incorrect
but it did display a sense of chivalry on the part of one
man, a sense of chivalry which was sadly lacking in many
English noble lords and officials in their dealings with the
men who came ashore from Armada ships.

CHAPTER THREE

THREE DANGEROUS HUMOURS

AT the centre of the web which was Queen Elizabeth's
method of government sat the Secretary of State, Francis
Walsingham. The slightest tremor at the periphery was
certain to be communicated to the man at the centre. To
him came the reports of spies and informers, of secretaries
of area councils, of governors and of sheriffs. It was a time
when the old unity of England had been broken. Out of
the Reformation grew a new ruling class, richer and more
powerful because of their seizure of Church lands. Side
by side with them grew men who were adventurers in
amassing wealth—in an era that would not be matched for
the excesses of free enterprise until many centuries later in
the United States of America. In a society which accepted
might as right, the neighbouring country of Ireland offered
prospects of land, wealth and power for second sons. So
it had become almost completely an appendage of England
save for parts of the North and North-West which provided fastnesses for the Irish and where it was dangerous
for Englishmen to enter.

Secretary Walsingham knew all this, but it must be
assumed that the condition of Ireland was the least of his
worries. He may have smiled wryly when he received a
report from Sir John Perrot, then Lord Deputy of Ireland

'These people,' Sir John wrote, 'are addicted to three
dangerous humours—papistry, change of government and
licentious liberty. The time of their readiness to attempt

what they will do is nearer hand than is perhaps imagined.'

It was a complaint that was to be re-echoed in different words through the corridor of the centuries by the representatives of England's monarchs who served in Ireland.

From Cork, the Attorney-General, Sir John Popham, wrote of his fears to Lord Burghley. 'The people in these parts,' he said, 'are dangerously affected towards the Spaniards, but thanks be to God, their power—by her Majesty's good means—is shorter than it had been.'

In the Ireland of those days there was a sociologist who gave more thought to ways and means of pacifying the Irish people than did his fellow-Englishmen. He was Sir William Herbert, a man of some culture, who held the then wildly unorthodox view that if English settlers grabbed land by force, they should, at least, have some sense of responsibility towards those whom they had dispossessed. Sir William believed, among other things, that if the dispossessed Irish were given homes which would provide some kind of meagre shelter they would become less lawless and more amenable to the rule of the Court of Gloriana.

He wrote: 'The mantle serveth unto the Irish as to a hedgehog his skin or to a snail her shell, for a garment by day and a house by night. It maketh them, with the continued use of it, more apt and able to live and lie out in bogs and woods where their mantle serveth them for a mattress and a bush for a bedstead, and thereby they are less addicted to a loyal, dutiful and civil life.'

Francis Walsingham must have smiled even more broadly when he read those words, for if Sir William Herbert was deeply concerned about methods of keeping the Irish 'loyal and dutiful' the Secretary of State was not. It was sufficient for the Secretary of State that Ireland was in such a condition that it could not be used as a base for an invasion of England, and that it should continue to provide the tax-tributes for the joint-stock company which England had become with Queen Elizabeth as symbol of authority and managing-director. At this point it is interesting to note

that through the centuries the policy of England towards
Ireland never changed and its two simple objectives were
always the same.

Francis Walsingham paid more attention to reports
which came from Ireland on certain happenings in Spain.
It appeared to be inevitable that the country and the empire
ruled by Philip II would one day clash with the nation of
trading adventurers who had been given almost a free hand
in a mixture of legitimate trade and piracy under the
Tudors.

Sir John Perrot, the Queen's Lord Deputy in Ireland, was
becoming nervous in January 1586, when he took his quill
and parchment to tell Walsingham: 'I hear by shipping
that came from Portugal to Waterford that the King of
Spain threateneth much, and is, as they say, prepareth
greatly to annoy England and Ireland, and we must prepare for this land better than is done.'

A few weeks later he was bemoaning the fact that there
had been no passage for more than a month across the
channel so that he could inform Walsingham that 'John
Challis, ship's captain, arrived at Cork to say that 20,000
from Spain were to land in Ireland in the spring.' Later
in the year he had even more alarming news to send to
London—'James Horre, of Waterford landed in a barque
to say that 300 sail of Spaniards started for Ireland under
command of the Duke of Alba, and afterwards were drawn
back again into Spain, and the King caused them to be
stayed and their men discharged for this time.' Sir John
repeated his warning that he had no money, he had a small
store of munitions, his soldiers were deserting, and he did
not trust the Irish if there were no means of keeping them
in check. Then he added: 'A Frenchman arrived in Galway
to say that in inner parts of Spain men, corn, armour and
munitions are preparing for invasion.' In almost every
dispatch from Dublin castle, Sir John was telling the man
at the centre of the web of Elizabeth's government that
England was in danger. News brought by an Irish mer-

chant who had been in Spain and in Portugal was faithfully
transmitted. The merchant said that the King of Spain was
preparing an invasion-army of 40,000, and in Lisbon the
merchant said he saw 'eighty-five great hulks towed up-
river and much munitions and armour amaking'.

Sir John, a dutiful servant of the Queen, thought that
the business of getting secret service information out of
Spain deserved a more professional approach. In February
1586, he wrote to Walsingham:

'I send over now a couple of spies that are fit men, I
think, and that will discover all the Spanish purposes. I
will shortly send you a cipher and a piece of parchment
indentured. When they write unto you by that character
and send the counterpart indenture you may know that
it cometh from them.'

It is tantalising that there is no record of what these
two intrepid practitioners of espionage sent back from
Spain—if they ever did get there, or if they used the
serrated-edged parchment to prove their identities. But the
Spanish war of nerves on England's rulers continued. It
was helped by an Irishman who had married a French girl
and who then had his home at Bayonne. He wrote a letter
to a relative in Waterford to say that part of a Spanish
army of invasion would arrive in Ireland in the spring of
1587. He had volunteered to join the Spanish force as a
means of re-visiting the scenes of his boyhood. Regret-
fully he had to say that his brothers-in-law looked with
disfavour on his intended departure from Bayonne and he
had to cancel his plans. The letter came into the hands of
the captain of the ship which arrived in Waterford and was
handed over to the Queen's officials. In turn, Sir John
Perrot sent it to Francis Walsingham.

As 1586 faded into 1587 Sir John's reports from Ireland
became more insistent. An escaped prisoner from Spain,
by name David Cole, landed at Galway to tell that Spanish
soldiers were being moved from all parts of Spain to Lisbon
and at Cadiz 'forty sail of Flemings were being provisioned

for invasion'. In the same month of April Walsingham had
a more authoritative report on his desk. It came from
Francis Drake, the legendary English sea-dog, who wrote:
'I assure your Honour that the like preparation was never
heard of nor known as the King of Spain hath and daily
maketh to invade England. His provisions of bread and
wine are so great as will suffice 40,000 men a whole year.'
In England the Privy Council ordered warning-beacons to
be prepared on the cliff-tops of the south coast and that
church bells should ring at the sight of the first mast-tip
of the Spanish invasion-fleet.

Assiduously attending to the business of his masters, Sir
John Perrot in May, 1588, transmitted more definite news
about the impending invasion when he was able to send
information that the King of Spain had issued a proclamation directing mobilisation of his mariners and soldiers at
Lisbon. This news came to Sir John in a roundabout
fashion which he described as coming from 'a man named
Russell from Drogheda, being in Biscay in Spain, spoke
with one, Byrne, who was waiting to get his goods cleared'.
Finally, on June 16, 1588, Sir John was able to tell Walsingham in a dispatch from Dublin: 'This present day there
came certain merchants of this town out of Bilbao who
were there these eleven days past. Whilst they were there,
there were great processions and invocations made for the
good success of the Spanish fleet.'

Sir John, no doubt, writing from the heart, added the
words: 'God send them all mischance.'

The mischance which Sir John so ardently desired for
the King of Spain's invasion forces had already fallen upon
Ireland. It was, indeed 'a most distressful country'. There
was little national outlook. Bitter feuds divided the earls
of Norman descent in the South, while in the North the
old-Irish chieftains seemed more intent on achieving per-
sonal supremacy than in forming a united force against the
English crown. It was a country which, in appearance, was
vastly different from that which we know today. The land

was swampy and undrained, small patches were cleared for
growing corn, dense thickets of brushwood covered the
surface. Only within the Pale was there a semblance of a
road system. Over the rest of the country there were narrow
paths which wandered around bogs, lakes and mountains.
There were few bridges, and river crossings were made at
places shallow enough to provide a ford. Life was primi-
tively simple. A form of oaten cake was staple food with
meat; the rivers gave salmon and trout, and there were reeds
for thatching little mud-walled houses. All that these people
asked was a means of subsistence—to stay alive was the
main purpose of their simple, pastoral life. It was a country
of sharp contrasts. There were also large areas—particularly
in Offaly—where lands were well-cultivated, heavily pop-
ulated, and where means of transport and of travel were
quite good.

In Irish school history books the historic facts are rarely
stressed that the Irish, who were in the pay of the Queen,
robbed, massacred, hanged, and handed over scores of
Spaniards to her Majesty's officers for summary and brutal
execution. Nor has it been stressed that in many of the
records which have survived, the Irish—in the opinion of
some Spaniards—were 'savages' and 'wild men'. Yet in
extenuation of all these things it must be recorded that the
Irish were a people living under a reign of terror. Just nine
years before the Spanish ships were wrecked on the Irish
coast the Desmond rising had been crushed with extreme
ferocity and cruelty. In counties Kerry, Limerick, Cork
and Waterford, the Desmond overlordship dated back to
the earliest days of the Norman invasion. The sixteenth
Earl of Desmond was no fighter, but his cousin, James
Fitzmaurice Fitzgerald, dreamed the old, old Irish dream
of throwing out the English with foreign aid. Thousands
perished in the suppression of that rising and Munster
became largely a waste land. The condition of the province
was, according to all the descriptions, frightful beyond
imagination. The herds of cattle had been swept away, the

earth had not been tilled and famine came to decimate what
the sword of the executioners had left. Rather casually
an English gentleman, writing from Cork, chronicled the
fact that in his neighbourhood 30,000 died from famine in
six months. It was but one of many accounts of the
appalling ruin in 'this most riche and plentiful countrie
full of corne and cattell'. Edmund Spenser, the poet who
was one of the English 'plantation' settlers, described
Munster: 'Out of every corner of the woodes and glinnes
they came creeping foorthe upon thyr handes, for thyr
legges could not bear them; they looked like anatomyes
of death, they speak like ghosts crying out of thyr graves
and they did eat of the dead carrions.' Lord Grey who
had directed the bloodstained repression of the rising was
recalled to London. He was in disfavour with the Queen
and with Lord Burghley, not because of his harsh measures,
but because taxation monies had fallen in Munster. Against
this it counted for nothing that '1,485 chief men and gentlemen were slain, not accounting those of meaner sort, nor
yet executions by law and the killing of churls which were
innumerable'. In the light of this grim record Lord Grey,
apparently, could not understand why he had got into the
bad books of the Queen and the Privy Council.

CHAPTER FOUR

THE KING DECIDES

FOR MORE than twenty years before the ships of the Spanish
Armada foundered on the reefs of the Irish coast it was
manifest that one day Spain and England would be at war.
Between these two nations there was a vendetta which
could end only in the survival of one or the other. In the
sixteenth century the power of Spain was gigantic. On land
the Spanish armies were formed of men who were inured
to fighting—well-trained, strictly disciplined and profession-

ally led. On sea, Spanish galleons had navigated the most
distant seas and had brought home to the national treasury
the riches of South America and of the West Indies. The
power of the Turks had been broken, and everywhere the
power of this mighty empire was feared. But in the west,
England was emerging as a challenger to the Spain of
King Philip II. The genius of the English for trade and
commerce was seeking an outlet, and for this island people
their skill and love of the sea presented a means by which
wealth, power and prestige could be obtained. The realisa-
tion that the destiny of England depended on the sea and
control of the sea did not come quickly. It was a slow
awakening, but Henry VIII, father of Queen Elizabeth,
formed the nucleus of the once-powerful British empire
when he spent vast sums for those days on ships of war.
The policy was carried on by Elizabeth, aided by merchants
who banded together to build, equip and provision trading
vessels which were heavily armed. The shipyards at
London, Bristol and Plymouth were building vessels of new
design and more seaworthy than those of any other nation.
When the 'cold war' between England and Spain was at
freezing point, Elizabeth could call upon a naval force of
about twenty galleons—fighting-ships that were the battle-
ships of the sixteenth century. These were the ships on
which a tradition would be built, culminating in 1911 when,
to celebrate the coronation of George V, the Royal Navy
gathered at Spithead in the biggest assembly of warships
in the world's history.

The King of Spain was a careful, prudent man who
calculated the effect of every important step he was called
upon to make. His industry in the control of his empire
was truly astonishing. So completely did he draw the lines
of power into his own hands that he became a one-man
civil service and a one-man army and naval staff. With
extreme care he played out his game of power-politics,
always shrewd, always far-seeing. But the historical fact
remains that the King of Spain's power and prestige rested

on a financial quicksand. The credit of the crown had never been lower. Most of its resources had been pledged to the bankers or the moneylenders. As a result of costly wars the King had had to make a humiliating declaration of bankruptcy. Weighed down with care, he must have greeted the years 1578–83 with some relief. He made a series of truces with the Turks and thus was freed from the risk of war in the Mediterranean. Next he completed the conquest of Portugal, and added the Portuguese maritime empire to his own. A new surge of purpose filled the conservative monarch. He had checkmated French hopes to gain Brazil, his conquest of Portugal now gave him the balance of power in the Atlantic. Yet he was still involved in war, for the Netherlands were in revolt against his rule. Suppression of the revolt was costly and did nothing to reduce the cost of bread in Spain.

The subtlety of English policy at this period is a good example of how it was to be moulded towards Europe down through the centuries. Queen Elizabeth wrote to her Privy Council: 'We think it good for the King of Spain to be impeached both in Portugal and his Islands and also in the Low Countries, whereto we shall be ready to give such indirect assistance as shall not at once be a cause of war.' England, in other words, should make as much trouble as it was possible to make for the King of Spain, preserve a balance of power in Europe which would suit England's interests, and allow English trade to increase. This policy, so long as it was allowed to operate, proved successful.

Yet the enormous wealth that lay virtually untapped in the New World made the eyes of English seafarers and merchants glint. Spain enforced a completely exclusive policy in respect of trade with its American and West Indian settlements. The men who had sailed there first were determined that what they had seized they would hold against all comers. In this attitude they were matched by the Portuguese, who, in their exploration and colonisation of settlements in the east, made it a rule of policy to allow no other traders in these territories. Like the cartels of this modern age they carved enormous trading areas for their exclusive use—Spain taking the west and Portugal the east. The Dutch and the French efforts to gain a trading foothold were contemptuously brushed aside by the men who ruled from Madrid and from Lisbon. But the English were more tenacious, more eager to take a part in a great expansion of opportunities to obtain wealth. Their eagerness was one of the chief causes of Philip's decision to crush this competition by open war against Queen Elizabeth's England. The King took a drastic step towards war when he seized all the English merchant ships in Spanish ports. Now completely convinced that with the annexation of Portugal the King of Spain planned a line of sea-bases which could neutralise, if not destroy, England's sea power, the Queen's Privy Council advised open intervention by England in the revolt of the Dutch against their Spanish master. The Earl of Leicester was sent with a large force of English soldiers to the Netherlands. The gauntlet was also thrown down in the acceptance by Leicester of the title governor-general which implied that Elizabeth claimed sovereignty of the Low Countries. This acceptance had a sequel which may be historically typical. Sir William Stanley had brought over a regiment of Irishmen to serve under Leicester. But when the Earl accepted the title of governor-general, Sir William Stanley went over to the Spanish side and the Irish fought ferociously against the English. It was thought that Sir William, who was styled 'the renegade', may have been among the castaways from the Armada on the Irish coast, and instructions were given about his possible identification.

The King of Spain's decision to crush England's power as a nation had also a political undercurrent. In Scotland the young King James, hoping to gain succession to the throne of England, signed a defensive alliance against

foreign powers with Queen Elizabeth. His action virtually
signed the death-warrant of his French-born mother, Mary
Queen of Scots. Elizabeth, now feeling confident that there
was nothing to fear from James of Scotland, consented to
the execution of his mother. Mary's death removed one of
the last obstacles to Philip's determination to deal with
those grasping English once and for all. If he had let the
years go by without taking action openly it was because
he did not wish to put a pro-French Queen on the throne
of England.

There was, too, a religious undercurrent. Elizabeth had
been excommunicated, and thus a war against England
could be fought with the cause of religion as justification.
The Armada was an example of how religious interests
and trading interests can be so intertwined in war that it
is well-nigh impossible to separate them and to attribute
more weight to one interest than to another. In the case
of Philip's decision the difficulty of separation is almost
impossible.

As Philip II pondered in his chamber in the centre of
the Escorial, the last straw which broke the back of his
normal caution must have come with news of Francis
Drake's bloodstained rampage of piracy against Spanish
possessions.

Drake, now a legendary figure of enormous magnitude
in the traditions and history of England, was the son of
a Puritan. He was a splendid seaman and a daring adven-
turer. In the summer of 1572 he had sailed to Panama.
This was the isthmus from which the Spaniards re-shipped
at Nombre de Dios the gold and silver from the mines of
Peru. Drake and his well-armed company landed at the
mouth of the Chagre river and raided the mule-trains which
were loaded with gold, pearls, rubies, emeralds, diamonds
and silver bars. The silver was too heavy to carry so,
Drake himself buried it in a secret place. Even today
men are still seeking that hidden hoard of silver, for Drake
never returned to recover it. Up and down the sun-

drenched coast he sailed, pillaging and burning the
unprotected settlements. He captured a galleon which
had sailed from Lima with the produce of a year's mining.
Her ballast was silver and her cargo was gold, emeralds
and rubies. There were twenty tons of silver bullion,
thirteen chests of silver coins and a hundredweight of gold.
The value of this cargo alone was enormous. In September,
1585, he again set out for the West Indies with a force of
2,500 men in twenty-five privateers. If the ships did not
fly the black flag with a skull and crossbones, there was
little doubt that they were pirates. It was a barefaced
commercial undertaking, financed by bankers and
merchants, and with the connivance of the Queen and
the Privy Council. Drake began by raiding the town of
Vigo where he robbed the church of everything that was
valuable and portable. The fleet then sailed to the Cape
Verde Islands where the settlement town was razed to
the ground. At St. Domingo, in the West Indies, he
burned half the town and agreed not to burn the other
half on payment of 25,000 ducats by the cowed inhabitants.
At Carthagena he extorted 30,000 ducats as his price for
sparing the population from a mass-hanging and the town
from destruction by fire. He returned after a circum-
navigation of the globe with holds filled with gold and
silver, jewels and spices and many exotic bales of silk. The
merchants and the bankers who were shareholders in the
venture were delighted with the return on their money.
Although the Queen and the Privy Council declined to
accept any responsibility for Drake's depredations, all of
them took a share of the spoils. In Spain there was
depression and a wringing of hands by merchants for
whom the supply of gold and silver from Peru and Mexico
had dried up. Many of them were ruined. The effect on
the shaky financial structure of the Spanish economy was
grievously serious.

This was an act of war in Spanish eyes. Philip at once
saw the danger. The Spanish empire would cease to exist

if the wealth which came from the west were to be pirated
by Englishmen. The King of Spain made his decision:
England would be invaded.

CHAPTER FIVE

THE INVINCIBLE FLEET

AROUND the fortress at Duncannon close to Waterford
there was a mesh of scaffolding. Masons worked to
strengthen the walls and carpenters laboured at the draw-
bridge and portcullis. The improvement and strengthening
of this defensive position seems to have been the only
positive step taken by the English to prepare for invasion
by Spain of Ireland. At the time there were only 1,761
English soldiers on the Irish list and their material was
in a truly wretched state. Guns had rusted and their
carriages were rotted. Supplies of powder and of arms
were everywhere deficient. There can be little doubt the
Privy Council of England believed that if Philip attacked
he would do so directly without wasting time in a prelim-
inary seizure of a part of Ireland. The work at Duncannon
may have been a token defensive gesture to allay the fears
of those English settlers who were none too happy in their
Irish surroundings.

In Spain the shipwrights swarmed over big ships, small
ships, pinnaces and squat store-vessels. The adze of the
coopers shaped staves for water-casks, and in the long
ropewalks strong cables were being twined for the great
fleet which the Spaniards called 'The Invincible Armada'.
From February to April in that fateful year of 1588 the
King of Spain had become obsessed with the idea that the
invasion of England should start as soon as possible.
The King was fortunate in having a willing servant in
Don Alvaro de Bazan, Marquis of Santa Cruz, to whom
he had entrusted the task of preparing and leading the

invasion-fleet. The Marquis was a strong character who had made his name famous at the sea-battle of Lepanto. He was sixty-two years of age, but he was still virile, active and clear-headed in his planning and in his decisions. There can be small doubt that in endeavouring to obey Philip's pressing directions to assemble a fleet at Lisbon he worked himself to death. The first estimate made by the Marquis of the number of ships, the number of men and the quantity of provisions, guns and munitions needed for the expedition may have been submitted in an effort to deter the King from carrying out his 'Enterprise of England'.

Santa Cruz asked for sixty first-line warships. He must have known that in all the wide-flung ports of the Spanish empire such a number could not be found. And even if these vessels were to be gathered at Lisbon, how could they be armed, provisioned and crewed in such a short time? He also specified, in addition, one hundred merchant ships converted to war-vessels or for transporting stores, mules and horses. They were nowhere to be found, but week by week the pressure from the King in the Escorial grew more intense. The gruelling work of preparation and the nagging anxiety took their toll of Santa Cruz. He became ill and within a few days he died at Lisbon on February 9, 1588.

Even with the hindsight of centuries it is not yet known why the King of Spain selected the Duke of Medina Sidonia as leader of his invasion-fleet in succession to Santa Cruz. The new leader—Don Alonso de Guzman el Bueno, Duke of Medina Sidonia and Captain-General of Andalusia, to give him his full titles—was no fool, but he was also no seaman or masterful leader of men. It was an amazing choice, for the Duke complained when informed of what his King desired of him that his health was not good, and that whenever he went to sea he became seasick and always caught cold. It would be difficult to imagine a less thrustful admiral of an invasion force. But the Duke went further in his pleas to be relieved of an unwelcome command. He wrote in a letter to the King that he knew nothing of what the Marquis of Santa Cruz had been doing, still less did he know anything of England. His letter added: 'I feel that I should give but a bad account of myself, commanding thus blindly, and being obliged to rely on the advice of others, without knowing good from bad, or which of my advisers might want to deceive or to displace me.' The Duke, in a final effort to change the King's command, pleaded that the Adelantado Major of Castile would make a better commander because he was a man of much experience in military and naval matters, 'and a good Christian, too'. It has been suggested that the Duke was selected because he was a wealthy man and that soldiers and sailors would sail with him, safe in the knowledge that they would be paid. This assumption cannot be correct for the Duke informed the King in the same letter: 'My family is burdened with a debt of nine hundred thousand ducats, and I cannot spend a *real* in your service.' But the King was adamant. Whether he was subject to seasickness or not, the Duke would lead the Armada. Reluctantly and heavy at heart, Medina Sidonia went to Lisbon to take over command.

There is a school of thought which advances the theory that the King was fully aware of the Duke's shortcomings but that he possessed one quality which the King favoured —the Duke would do what his royal master told him to do. For guidance in seamanship he would have the most experienced seamen of the empire to serve under him, and for second-in-command there would be Don Diego de Valdez, a taciturn veteran of many ocean-voyages. And so the die was cast—a man who had never sailed in the waters of the English Channel went to Lisbon to become supreme commander of a force of 130 ships, 8,000 seamen, 19,000 soldiers, with grandee and hidalgo volunteers, officers, chaplains, surgeons, galley-slaves—at least 3,000 more. He had to direct the provisioning of this vast war effort, make certain that it was efficiently and sufficiently supplied with guns great and small, and with powder to service them. He had to inspect hulls, spars, cordage and canvas and he had to make the acquaintance of the naval and military captains he had been called upon to lead in the greatest sea enterprise the world had ever known up to that time. The fleet was organised on a military basis in squadrons, taking into account the tonnage of the vessels and their spread of canvas. It was necessary to sub-divide them into this military-style formation because the Armada force was composed of sailors and soldiers of different nationalities—Spanish, Italian, Dalmatians and Guipuzcoans. And, of course, there had to be many Irishmen among the men who crowded the decks of the fleet. Some of their names have been recorded— John Brown, of Clontarf; Patrick Roynane, of Limerick; John Burnell, of Drogheda; James MacGarry, of the Cross in Tipperary; John Lynch, a master-gunner; William Brown, a mariner; Edmond Eustace, Cahill MacConnor and Henry O'Mulryne—all sailed under the Duke of Medina Sidonia, some of them to die and some of them destined to return to Spain.

Two members of the Desmond family, Don Mauricio and Don Tomas Fitzgerald, as they were described in Spanish lists, were on board one of the vessels which was wrecked off the Scottish coast. With another Irishman, Thomas Aspolle, they were among the survivors of the wreck. The son of James Fitzmaurice was less fortunate. He died at sea in one of the ships which sought shelter on the Irish coast. An Irish friar, James Ne Dowrough, was among those who landed from a wreck on the coast of Donegal. He escaped the clutches of the search-parties sent to capture him and he lived out his life in Ireland. These Irishmen were among the crowds who crowded the streets of Lisbon when, in the cathedral, Mass was celebrated by the Archbishop of Lisbon who asked for a benediction on the fleet and the men who sailed on this

dangerous expedition. The standard of the Duke of
Medina Sidonia was blessed and then carried to a convent
of Dominican nuns where it was placed over the altar.

On May 4, 1588, the ships of the Invincible Armada
moved slowly down the brown waters of the Tagus. On
the 18th of that month mainsails were shaken out and
the fleet sailed on its voyage of historic destiny. In essence,
its mission was simple—as all plans for great and daring
enterprises should be. The task of the Duke of Medina
Sidonia was to sail to a point off Dunkirk to act as
protecting escort to an army which would be shuttled
across the Channel to invade England. The army was
under the command of Alexander Farnese, Duke of Parma,
a soldier of brilliant talents who had all but completed
his task of subduing the rebellious Lowlanders. He had
welded a hotch-potch of mercenaries into a well-trained
and disciplined instrument of war, and in his strategy and
in his tactics he had outmanoeuvred his less skilful
adversary, the Prince of Orange. At the core of his army
was a veteran division of Spanish infantrymen, soldiers
from boyhood to whom fighting was a way of life. And,
of course, among his soldiers were hundreds of Irish—
members of a Celtic people to whom war was as attractive
as it was to the swarthy-visaged Spaniards with whom in
temperament they had much in common. In all, the Duke
of Parma had an army of 60,000 of which more than
3,000 were cavalry.

The King's master-plan instructed the Duke of Medina
Sidonia that his principal task was to convoy the Duke
of Parma's army to the English shores. Unless it became
absolutely unavoidable he was not to engage in a naval
battle with the English fleet. When Parma's forces had
been shepherded across the Channel, then the Duke would
be free to settle accounts with the Queen's navy. It was
a plan which might have worked if the preparations had
been shrouded in the utmost secrecy. Instead of conceal-
ment, there was a laying bare of Spanish intentions long

before the fleet sailed on its mission of war. A report was prepared by the Duke of Medina Sidonia listing every ship in his fleet, the tonnage, its armament and its purpose in the coming attack. Details of this report were copied and within weeks it was being read in many of the capital cities of Europe with great interest. A copy of the report quickly found its way to London. At Greenwich, Francis Walsingham and Lord Burghley studied its details. The report contained a number of deliberate exaggerations of strength in numbers, soldiers, sailors and armament, and as its contents spread from city to city and port to port, there were inevitably additions made by those who passed on the news. In this way the Queen and her Privy Council were obligingly forewarned of Philip's intentions. The best that can be said about this is that the King and the Duke of Medina Sidonia were extraordinarily naive to believe it would cause such apprehension and terror among their enemies that they would fear to attack the Armada. All it did was to hurry on the preparations which the English were making to repel the invaders.

The King of Spain had not learned the lesson which has been learned by other nations who sought to violate the territory of England—that command of the sea is an essential to invasion of that sceptred isle. On the high hills which close around Boulogne there is a tall monument which marks the spot on which Napoleon Buonaparte stood as he contemplated an attack across the Channel on England. That narrow ditch of water is a bulwark against invasion. Napoleon turned away from the Channel. Later the Grand Fleet of Kaiser Wilhelm was to discover that it was impossible to win supremacy at sea against the descendants of Drake, Hawkins and Frobisher. Still later, Adolf Hitler went to Cap Griz Nez to look through a powerful range-finder at the white cliffs of Dover over the grey expanse of less than twenty miles of water which is England's shield. He, too, turned away. The invasion barges of The Third Reich, which lay in the same ports as those which sheltered the invasion-craft of the Duke of Parma many centuries before, were never used for the purpose the Fuehrer intended them to be used. The conception of England as an impregnable fortress, incapable of being invaded until the attacker had won command of the sea, lost its validity on the day the French airman, Bleriot, flew over those twenty miles of Channel to land on the cliffs of Dover. Henceforth it would be those nations who had supremacy and complete command of the air who would be sufficiently strong to impose their will by armed strength.

The King of Spain's invasion-plan took no account of the complexities of wind, currents, shoals and headlands which would confront the leader of his Armada. The English Channel is, even today, regarded by experienced seamen as a stretch of water in which skill and care must be exercised. It is a Channel in which the tides rise and fall from thirty to forty feet. In their ebbing and flowing they create powerful currents. The compressed waters are more often than not swept by strong winds that form a sea most dreaded by sailors—a series of powerful wave crests that succeed one another at short intervals. For Philip's fleet all these rapidly changing conditions awaited. They were to play a part in the failure of the enterprise which depended so much on brilliant seamanship. But the man who led the Armada was no sailor. For this lack of knowledge and skill in seamanship the Spaniards were to pay dearly.

CHAPTER SIX

THE ILL-STARRED BEGINNING

LED BY the Duke of Medina Sidonia in his flagship, the *San Martin*, which had been double-timbered with oak to make her hull invulnerable to cannon-fire, the mighty

Armada moved slowly down the Tagus, and by May 10, 1588, all the ships were concentrated at Belem. Santa Cruz had warned of the danger which lay in a late start. Now in his grave, his forecast that the fleet might be met by the north trade wind was proved to be accurate. Day by day the fleet drifted to leeward, making tortuously slow progress because the speed of the fastest ship had to be that of the slowest. As the fleet beat slowly down the coast it was, indeed, a manifestation of the maritime power of the Spanish empire. Sixty-five heavily-armed galleons and converted merchantmen led the line with twenty-five *urcas* (store-ships) close behind, followed by more than thirty light *pataches* or *zabras* and four galleasses. These galleasses were unusual inasmuch as they were propelled by sail, but in battle they could also be propelled by oarsmen. The oars gave them a manoeuvrability so lacking in vessels which relied only on sail.

The unfavourable winds continued to slow the advance of the fleet, and, in fact, a fortnight passed before Finisterre was sighted. Trouble was already beginning to loom. Many hundredweights of provisions were found to be rotten. Watercasks when broached were found to contain water that was undrinkable. Then came an outbreak of dysentery. In a conference with his captains, the Duke decided to make for the port of Corunna to replenish stores. Most of the fleet got safely into the shelter of the harbour or its headlands before darkness fell on Sunday, June 19. Those ships that remained outside were unlucky. Suddenly a fierce gale from the south-west began to blow, scattering the vessels which were forced to run before its fury. The gale did not last long, but valuable time had been lost before the Armada was able to regroup. This was an ill-starred beginning.

Two of the ships which ran before the storm were to seek shelter many days later along the Irish coast. The first was the *San Juan,* commanded by Juan Martinez de Recalde. The second was *La Rata Santa Maria Encoronada,*

under the command of Don Alonso Martinez de Leyva.
These two were brave, adventurous men. They rode out
the gale and after a day or so rejoined the fleet at Corunna.
They were in time for a council of war in which it became
evident that the resolution of the Duke of Medina Sidonia
to press on with the invasion of England had considerably
waned. The Duke had written to the King explaining that
the storm had scattered most of the fleet and that some of
the vessels might have foundered. He explained how
provisions and food had been found to be putrid. As
gently as he could make the suggestion, he put it to the
King that the enterprise should be called off. A pinnace
brought the Duke's letter to the King. In reply the Duke
was informed that it was the King's command that he
should follow instructions. For four weeks the Armada
remained at Corunna taking in fresh supplies, repairing
the storm damage to the ships and putting right a host
of defects which had become apparent since the departure
from Lisbon. With fresh food and water, dysentery ended.
Ashore, the sailors and soldiers gained new enthusiasm.
The losses of the fleet in the storm had been nil. One
by one the vessels straggled back to Corunna, were
re-provisioned and their crews rested. When the order was
given to set sail once again there was more optimism
among those thousands of soldiers and sailors than there
had been at their departure from Lisbon. The date was
July 12. The Armada streamed across the Bay of Biscay
with a fair wind for the mouth of the Channel.

To England had come a flood of reports telling of the
preparations for the invasion. It would be natural to
expect that the Queen and her Privy Council would be
spending every moment in making the navy ready for the
great test of strength that lay ahead. But the contrary
was the case. It had been a severe winter, with many gales
and heavy rain. Many of the galleons were laid-up at
their ports.

In December the Queen had ordered the fleet to be

paid-off at Chatham. In governing the country, Elizabeth used a parsimony which was remarkable. The cut-back on the naval force drove the Lord Admiral, Lord Howard of Effingham, almost to breaking-point. Only after the strongest pressure had been exerted did the Queen allow half the fleet to be re-commissioned. The Queen, and, perhaps, the majority in the Privy Council, were convinced that war with Spain could be staved off. And certainly the King of Spain and the Duke of Parma did their best to lull the English into that happy state of optimism. This belief was strengthened when news of the death of Santa Cruz reached London. There were reports that the ships of the Armada were dispersing. The Duke of Parma let it be known that he would try to arrange some sort of peace conference with the English, knowing that Elizabeth preferred conferences to warfare. Even in Madrid the reports of diplomats accredited to Spain showed uncertainty about the King's objective in assembling his great fleet. With the coming of March the news from Spain became more grim. Yet the Queen gave no sign that she knew her crown and the land she ruled were in danger. Four of the finest ships in the navy were lying unmanned at Chatham—the *Triumph*, the *Victory*, the *Elizabeth Jonas*, and the *Bear*. Only at the last moment did Elizabeth give way to the pleadings of the Lord Admiral and put them into service. Although she did yield, she exercised her miserly talents in other ways. She allotted only enough money to provision the ships until the end of June—and no more was to be allowed. The result of all this pro-crastination and penny-pinching was to make the English fleet weaker than it should have been. The crews had been hastily pressed into service. They were badly clothed and badly fed. Worse still, the beer served to them was sour. The fleet had provisions for four weeks. By a reduction of rations these could be extended to serve six weeks. At the end of that time it was unlikely that the Queen would sanction any further expenditure. At the time when the Duke of Medina Sidonia ordered the Armada of Spain to sail out of Corunna the English fleet had half-rations for a week and powder and shot for about two days' fighting. England, as she has done so often in her history, was 'muddling through' the crisis and the alarums of war.

The pattern of 'muddling through' was repeated on land. The formation of a large army to repel the veteran soldiers of the Duke of Parma would be met by amateur volunteers whisked from the fields into the Queen's service. The names of a hundred thousand Englishmen prepared to defend their homes against the Spaniards had been listed. The assembly-points had been planned—but that was all. There were no reserves, no armaments that could be distributed on a large scale. Every man would have to arm himself. There were no stores of provisions, no tents. To lead this hotch-potch of a defence force the Queen chose the Duke of Leicester who could be counted to give her the deepest loyalty. As a soldier and a daring leader of men he was about the worst choice the Queen could have made. Leicester had not a great deal of experience as a soldier. He was noted for the way in which he alienated friendship and discarded advice, and at least one historian has given his opinion that the Duke regarded his rank as more than offsetting his military inexperience. Sir John Norris, a soldier of vast experience, had returned from the Netherlands campaign declaring that never again would he serve under the command of Leicester.

It was in this situation of unpreparedness that news came to London that the mighty Armada of Spain had been sighted at the mouth of the Channel. Once more bad weather slowed the speed of the invasion. The wind shifted to the north, then backed to the west from which quarter it began to blow a half-gale. The smaller ships ran for the shelter of French ports. The galleons and the great ships—which were converted merchantmen—stood-off and waited for the storm to subside. For two days the Armada was vulnerable to an attack by the English fleet—but no English sail was seen and once more it re-formed. The formation in which this great attacking force sailed had been carefully planned. It sailed in the form of a great crescent, the horns of which trailed on either flank for a distance of seven miles. In the centre sailed the Duke of Medina Sidonia in the *San Martin*. The squadron of Juan Martinez de Recalde covered the rear.

The Channel was still choppy after the near-gale when the Duke sent off two fast pinnaces—one to carry the news of his arrival in the Channel to the Duke of Parma, the second reporting his whereabouts to the King. That night the Spaniards saw the warning-beacons blazing along the English coast. Now England was awake to her danger. One of the most decisive sea-battles in the history of the world was about to begin.

Cautiously the Armada sailed slowly up-Channel with reduced sail. There was no sign of the English fleet. The crew of a captured fishing vessel gave the information that the enemy fleet had sailed from Plymouth. In the light of the moon the Spanish look-outs high on the fore-masts saw sails pass like ghosts between them and the dim shore-line. Were these the ships of Drake, of Seymour, of Howard? There was no way of knowing. At this point there is some evidence that the Duke-commander was urged to attack Plymouth, capture whatever ships he might find there, and use it as a base to which he could safely convoy the army of the Duke of Parma. But the Duke held strictly to the orders given to him by Philip. Indeed, most experts in naval warfare believe that he was wise in resisting the urging of his commanders who made the plea that offensive action was needed against Plymouth. He would have entered the harbour not knowing what forces he might meet there, the strength of the shore-guns, and unaware of the exact position of the English fleet. He could have run into a trap that would have meant annihilation for his proud ships. The Armada sailed on.

When dawn came the Armada was a little west of the Eddystone. Eleven English vessels were seen seeking to recover the wind, and towards the land forty others, big and small. This was the first sight the Spaniards were to see of their adversaries. The eleven ships were the squadron commanded by Lord Howard. Those closer to land were those led by Francis Drake—now Sir Francis Drake in reward for his piracy in the West Indies. The Spaniards sailed to the attack, the English swept across the horns of the defensive crescent, smoke spurting from the cannon on their decks. The engagement did not result in great damage to either fleet. The *San Juan de Portugal,* commanded by de Recalde, was damaged but she was extricated from a dangerous situation by the *Gran Grin,* one of the great ships which perished on the Irish coast. Twenty were killed on de Recalde's ship, a section of the rigging had been shot away and two cannon-balls had weakened the main-mast.

The action lasted until four in the afternoon. With great skill in seamanship, the Spaniards kept their crescent formation. It was a formation which had undoubtedly baffled the Englishmen who were eager to attack but were always in doubt about the point where they should make their main effort. Then disaster struck one of the great Spanish galleons. The *San Salvador,* vice-flagship of the Andalusian squadron, was shattered by an explosion. At one moment she was keeping perfect station in the formation. In the next, she was wallowing in the choppy sea and trailing a plume of smoke that had followed the explosion. The most likely explanation is that the explosion was the result of great carelessness in the handling of the powder-kegs in her magazine.

There have been stories that the disaster was caused by a Flemish gunner in revenge for punishment ordered by the commander. This account says that the gunner laid a trail to a powder-keg and then jumped overboard before the ship's planking was shattered by the blast. Whatever

the cause, two hundred were killed on the stricken ship
and the deck was blown into splinters.

The Duke of Medina Sidonia reacted quickly. Two
galleasses were ordered to take the *San Salvador* in tow.
This they did, and slowly they brought the vessel into the
safety of the formation. The anxiety of the Duke to save
the *San Salvador* is understandable. On board was the
Paymaster-General and it is believed that the ship carried
a huge fortune in ducats and in gold.

The Spaniards were to suffer another misfortune. This
time it concerned the Andalusian galleon *Nuestra Senora
de Rosario,* commanded by Pedro de Valdez, and with a
complement of 500 men. The vessel was one of the finest
in the fleet. In turning to help another vessel under attack
she collided with the *Santa Catalina* and broke her bowsprit
and foretopmast. As the ships moved apart it was seen
that *Nuestra Senora del Rosario* was unmanageable. An
attempt to take her in tow failed and eventually the galleon
was allowed to fall into the hands of the English. The
Duke of Medina Sidonia had to make a quick decision.
He could have ordered a section of the fleet to protect
the stricken vessel. He decided otherwise. The *Nuestra
Senora del Rosario* fell further astern and none of the
commanders was allowed an attempt at rescue.

On board she had a large sum of money and a box of
jewel-hilted swords which were intended as gifts from the
King of Spain to the Catholic peers of England who were
expected to aid the Spanish invasion. The desertion by
the Duke of Medina Sidonia of Pedro de Valdez and his
galleon caused great anger among the other squadron
commanders, but in the circumstances of the battle it
may be harsh to blame the Duke for his decision. Better
to lose one vessel than to break that tight formation.

That evening at sunset the fleets were off Portland.
Once more the English fleet attacked. The boom of the
cannon echoed over the water but the Armada sailed on.
The armament of both sides was primitive compared with

modern artillery. The cannon fired a ball which was not likely to cause a great deal of damage unless it could bring down masts or rigging. Accuracy was a matter of luck more than of good judgment. In the case of the English, the fleet fought under the handicap of the parsimony of their Queen. At the end of the action off Portland the English gunners had reached the end of their supply of gun-powder. Two days' supply, the Queen had estimated, should be sufficient to sink those marauding Spaniards. Now, however, the danger in which England stood had been clearly seen and fresh supplies of powder and provisions were rushed to Weymouth for shipment to the fleet. In this the English had the advantage of a shorter line of supply, but it was an advantage which was never exploited to the full. On board the *San Martin* the Duke of Medina Sidonia was receiving reports that powder and shot were running low. On he sailed with the English fleet trailing that unbreakable crescent. It was inevitable that one of the Spanish fleet should fall out of the formation. For a reason which none of the records disclose, the *Gran Grifon*, flagship of the squadron of store-ships, became a straggler. Almost at once she was surrounded by English galleons which sent shot after shot into her hull. She fought back gallantly and regained the safety of the formation—but not before many of her crew had been killed or wounded.

Up to this point it would appear that the English fleet was somewhat daunted by the sheer size of the Armada, and that Howard and Drake were content to pick off stragglers rather than risk a full-scale engagement with the Spaniards. There were actions against the Spanish rearguard, but at no stage was battle joined in such a way as to give a decisive result. Thus the two fleets sailed until they were off the eastern tip of the Isle of Wight. At this stage the Duke of Medina Sidonia must have felt satisfied that he had accomplished the first part of his mission with some degree of success. True, he had casualties. In one

day sixty men had been reported killed. He had lost one
fine ship through accident to the English, and another
galleon was a mere hulk. Nevertheless, his force was
otherwise intact and the English showed no sign of depart-
ing from their shadowing tactics. His next step would be
to make contact with the Duke of Parma to whom he had
already sent off two pinnaces to tell him of his position
in the Solent. He also included a plea to Parma to send
out a supply of round-shot in which the fleet was now
sadly deficient. He had plenty of powder, but without
the round-shot the next engagement with the English
could prove disastrous for Spain. The Duke of Medina
Sidonia was under the impression that the Duke of Parma
had his army encamped on the French coast and ready to
embark at a moment's notice in a fleet of barges. When
the two forces made contact it would then be the moment
to sweep those Englishmen from the Channel and to
proceed with the invasion of England.

If the hopes of the Duke of Medina Sidonia were high
they were matched by those of the English leaders. On
the deck of his flagship, Lord Howard touched the blade
of his sword on the shoulders of Hawkins and Frobisher,
creating them knights, a power which he possessed as Lord
Admiral of the Queen's fleet. The arrival of supplies of
provisions, of shot and powder made the outlook of the
English more promising. They looked forward to the
next engagement with the Armada, an engagement which
could no longer be delayed.

CHAPTER SEVEN

THE DISPERSAL BY FIRE

ALL DAY the Armada sailed with the English fleet astern.
The Spanish pilots steered for Calais Roads and as they

closed the French coast sails were struck and anchors
splashed in the water. The same orders were given in the
ships of the English fleet and so, as dusk fell over the
Channel, the Spaniards and the English swung at anchor
within sight of the high cliffs of Calais. Messengers sped
from the Duke of Medina Sidonia to the Duke of Parma.
The news with which they returned brought consternation
and dismay to the leaders of the Spanish fleet. They learned
that instead of being at Dunkirk to receive a signal to
launch his army against England, the Duke of Parma was
at Bruges many miles inland. And what was worse, Parma
sent a message expressing his pleasure at the safe arrival
of the Armada, but explaining it would be quite impossible
for him to play his part in the invasion until at least six
days of further preparation were to elapse. The messengers
sent by Medina Sidonia reported that all they had seen
at Dunkirk—which was thirty miles from Calais—was a
collection of unseaworthy barges. Certainly no effort was
being made to prepare for the embarkation of thousands
of soldiers. Now the plight of the Armada was perilous
indeed. After a week of running battle, with supplies
nearing exhaustion and with many of his fleet officers
weary from lack of sleep, the Duke of Medina Sidonia
had anchored in an exposed roadstead where the currents
were notoriously dangerous. And about a mile away the
English waited like birds of prey, unwilling to attack while
the Spaniards remained in the neutral waters of France—
a country which might side with Spain if there were an
affront by the English. The experienced sea-men of the
Armada tested the wind and hoped that it would not
veer to the north-west—a wind which would drive them
on to the shoals and sandbanks that lay close under their lee.

In the situation in which the men of Spain found themselves there was an element of farce. For months the
planning of this juncture of fleet and army had been
proceeding. The last detail had been settled. Letters had
come almost daily from the King to Parma. The Duke

of Medina Sidonia had kept his Majesty fully briefed on
his progress, by couriers despatched in fast-sailing fly-
boats. Now the fleet was being asked to swing at anchor
until the Duke of Parma was ready to play his part. It
is little wonder that the Armada leaders lost a great deal
of their confidence, and that the men they led should suffer
a lowering of morale. The explanation appears to be that
the Duke of Parma had come to the conclusion that the
plan was unworkable until complete naval supremacy
had been obtained for Spain in the Channel. This battle-
experienced leader of men knew that just outside the port
of Dunkirk a Dutch fleet was waiting to pounce on the
barges and light craft in which it was planned to make
the crossing to England. Without armament, the light-
weight fleet would be destroyed within a few hours. Besides,
his transport problems were well-nigh insuperable. Many
of the barges were rotten, others that were designed for
canal-traffic had a ridiculously low freeboard for a crossing
of the Channel. The number of experienced seamen
available to crew this extraordinary invasion-fleet was too
low. It is difficult to avoid the judgment that Parma
sincerely hoped the Armada would sail home and abandon
an enterprise which was doomed to failure. When the
Armada had departed he would get on with his task of
closing an iron hand around those troublesome people
of the Low Countries who resisted the rule of Spain. He
did not intend to allow the Dutch to massacre his fine
army on the waters of the Channel—a massacre they
would be only too pleased to carry out in revenge for the
stern and sometimes brutal methods of the Spanish leader
in crushing the revolt in the Netherlands. In the history
of the great battles of the world there cannot be found a
parallel for this tragi-farce which was played out in those
summer days of 1588 off the coast of France—days when
the destinies of two powerful nations were to be shaped
for many centuries.

That evening a council of war was held on board one

of the English galleons. Howard, Drake, Seymour, Hawkins
and Frobisher gathered around a table to plan their next
move. Little time was wasted and their decision was
taken with speed. After sunset a powerful flood-tide
would begin to sweep along the shore. On this tide fire-
ships could be floated into the centre of the Spanish ships.
It was a stratagem of naval warfare which had been used
before—now it might work again. An English pinnace
was sent on the dangerous mission of approaching the
Armada to report on its exact position. Meanwhile orders
were given to prepare the fire-ships, old vessels that could
be most easily spared. Pitch was poured on their decks
and plastered on their rigging. Intrepid sailors who would
steer them to a point near the Spanish ships were selected
and briefed in their task. They were to set fire to the
eight ships simultaneously, clamber down their sides and
return in the dinghies which they towed.

The Duke of Medina Sidonia had prepared for such
an attack. He had ordered several ships of light draught
to act as a screen. Smaller boats were sent to help them.
The oarsmen were given grappling irons and cables by
which they could divert any fire-ships which the English
might send floating towards the fleet. The Duke told his
captains that the screen would probably be effective. If,
by chance, any fire-ship threatened to reach the centre
of the Armada, the captains would buoy their anchors
and stand out to sea. The night was moonless—ideal
from the English point of view. A slight westerly wind
was blowing, a wind which fitted perfectly into the plan
of the English. Look-outs on the Spanish vessels quickly
saw eight ghostlike vessels moving towards them. Closer
and closer drifted the phantom ships. Orders were shouted
from ship to ship of the Armada, in Spanish, in Italian
and in French. With a whoosh of flame one of the drifting
ships became a burning mass—then another, and another.
In the glare the Spanish ships stood out starkly against
the shoreline and the surface of the anchorage was crim-

soned. Two of the Duke's small ships drew two of the
fire-ships off course, but the other six—quite close together
—drifted on.

It must be remembered that in the dispersal of the
Armada which followed there was the factor of fear. Fire
was dreaded by seamen of the sixteenth century. Their
vessels were vulnerable to the fire-ships. The captains
acted as one man. They shouted orders to cut or to buoy
their anchor cables, and swiftly they fell away from the
danger on the strong current. For those lost anchors
many thousands of Spaniards were to pay a fearful price
when, many days later, they sought shelter along the coast
of Ireland. They could never return to Calais to recover
the anchors. More than one hundred anchors were left
at Calais Roads.

The break-up of the Spanish formation was the result
most desired by the English commanders. The plan
succeeded, although not a single Spanish vessel came in
contact with the fire-ships. All of them drifted ashore to
burn themselves down to the water-line. Two miles outside
the harbour, the Duke of Medina Sidonia in the *San
Martin* watched the dawn come. He was satisfied that
quick action had defeated the purposes of the fire-ships,
but as the sky grew brighter he discovered that his fleet had
been divided. Only forty of his biggest ships were riding
at their sheet-anchors close to him. The remainder had
drifted to leeward and were dangerously near the shore
at Gravelines. They could not rejoin the flagship because
of the set of the wind and the tide. If the Duke were to
sail towards them the entire fleet might run aground on
the shelving banks. Already there had been the loss of
the galleass *San Lorenzo*. She ran ashore, her commander,
Hugo de Moncada, was killed, but some of the crew
swam or waded to land and to safety.

In the battle which followed, the English leaders changed
their tactics. Sailing closer to their enemies—much closer
than they had dared to do in previous encounters, their

cannon caused great damage and many deaths. The *San Martin* seems to have been in the thick of the fight. She was so riddled that the pumps could not keep pace with the onrush of water, and for some time it was thought that she would founder. But working under great difficulties, her crew repaired the worst shot-holes and she sailed on.

The galleon *San Mateo* was less fortunate. She, too, was badly holed. Drifting with wind and tide, she ran ashore near Ostend where she was attacked by three Dutch vessels. The commander of the *San Mateo* was a brave man. For three hours he repelled every attempt by his attackers to gain a footing on his tilted decks. Then he surrendered to be led off to captivity. His crew fared worse. All of them were massacred.

The next victim of the English guns was the galleon *San Felipe* which drifted ashore at Nieuport, a port fortunately held by the Spaniards.

Next to go was the *Maria Juan,* a Biscayan great ship with Pedro de Ugarte in command. Slowly she began to sink while two vessels of her squadron sailed close to her. Only one boat-load of men left the stricken ship before she suddenly lurched and sank, taking close on 300 men with her. It brought the total of Spanish losses to 600 killed and 800 wounded on this single day. Five Spanish ships had been lost as a result of collisions, one had blown up, another had been captured, and at Gravelines three were lost as the result of the pounding of English guns.

The English loss in ships had been nil. Their casualties in dead and wounded totalled a mere one hundred. From the point of view of losses and casualties, the battle off Gravelines was an undoubted English vistory. Towards the end of the battle the Spanish broadsides grew fewer and fewer. Supplies of shot were almost exhausted. Each galleon commander sought to evade action to conserve ammunition. If they had only known it, the English were in a similar plight, and the battle ended because neither side was able to continue. As night drew near the English fleet parted with the Armada and stood off for two miles, confident that with the vicious north-wester which had begun to blow, morning would find the proud Armada wrecked on the shoals towards which the wind was slowly but surely pressing them.

Gradually the wind rose until it was blowing a near-gale. This was a supreme test of seamanship for the Spaniards. The fact that none of their ships ran upon the shoals is sufficient proof that they were skilled sailors. When morning came the Spanish fleet was still intact with the faithful Juan Martinez de Recalde and de Leyva close to the flagship of the Duke of Medina Sidonia. In the cold light of the dawn English and Spaniards looked across the strip of turbulent sea which separated them.

In the first light of the new day it was seen that nothing had changed. The Spanish ships were clawing to keep themselves off the sandy shore. The English kept steady station, menacingly watchful. But the menace was illusory. Without powder or shot, the biggest English ships were harmless. Drake wrote afterwards: 'We were resolved to put on a brag and to go on as if we needed nothing.' The bluff was successful. It was also justified because it seemed that it would be only a matter of hours before the Armada would be driven ashore. The *San Martin* had only six fathoms beneath her keel. Other ships closer to the shore-line signalled that they were afloat in only five fathoms.

Among the Spaniards there was grim determination to sell their lives dearly. Wind and tide had forced them into an impossible situation. Suddenly their plight was dramatically changed—the wind backed to south-south-west, and as it held from that quarter they could ease their sheets and steer into the Channel with white water again tumbling at their bows. The wind enabled the separated ships to reform, and in that crescent formation they would be almost immune from a full-scale attack. The English watched them sail north—confident that so long as they held that course the danger of making contact with Parma's army would recede with every league that passed beneath their keels. Yet there was another possibility. The Armada might sail to a Scottish port. There the fleet could receive shelter and replenishment of their supplies from Scottish Catholics who would, perhaps, welcome Spanish aid in exacting revenge for the execution of Mary. But the Duke of Medina Sidonia had no such plan. A council of war was held on the flagship. It was decided that if the wind changed, the fleet would fight its way back through the Straits. But the wind held, and the mighty Armada bore northwards never to return. The English followed until with food and water running out they were forced to sail into the Firth of Forth. It was August 2, 1588. Few of those who perished on the coast of Ireland had an inkling of their fate as they sailed into the cold, grey northern waters.

CHAPTER EIGHT

A CAPTAIN REPRIEVED

THE DUKE of Medina Sidonia had failed his royal master. If he had been a seaman of long experience the story of the Armada might have been different. But although some students of his leadership have rated him a fool, the available facts show that he was a man of determination when ruggedness was needed. As the fleet sailed north he realised that discipline of the sternest kind would be needed if the ships he commanded were to be brought back safely to Spain. Officers in pinnaces were sent to inform all captains that formation must be kept, and that on no account was any vessel to sail ahead of the flagship. This was a repetition of an order which he had given when the Armada was off Portland. Those who disobeyed the order would be hanged. To Francisco de Bobadilla,

Major-General commanding all the soldiers in the fleet, he gave the task of ensuring that his order would be carried out. The Major-General who was, of course, a landsman, must have been glad to get some form of activity in which his authority could be exercised. It would have been doubly welcome if it gave him an opportunity of dealing with those mariners who seemed to have baulked the Major-General of winning battle honours against the English because of faulty seamanship—or so it appeared to the high-ranking soldier.

The Duke of Medina Sidonia's order was to have unfortunate results for the captain of the *San Pedro,* one of the smaller vessels of the Armada. He was Francisco Cuellar who later wrote down in some detail what befell him. He said: 'The *San Pedro* had suffered badly from gun-shots and immediate repairs were made, but still water kept coming in. While I was exhausted and taking some rest—not having had rest and little sleep for ten days—the mate spread sail and forged about two leagues ahead of the flagship so as to be able to make repairs. At the moment he was about to furl sail a despatch-boat came alongside with orders from the Duke that I was to go on board the flagship at once.'

Seething with rage at the degradation to which he had been subjected, Captain Cuellar clambered up the side of the flagship and was at once brought to the cabin where de Bobadilla sat awaiting his coming. The trial was swift. The Major-General ordered that Cuellar should be taken to the ship on which sailed the Auditor-General of the Armada, Martin de Aranda, and he was to be there hanged.

This was a curious decision. Not long before Cuellar had been summoned to the flag-ship, another court-martial had been held on Don Cristobal de Avila who had been accused of the same disregard of orders. The sentence of death was pronounced as swiftly by de Bobadilla— Cristobal de Avila would die by hanging. Although he was a nobleman, and a neighbour of the Duke of Medina

Sidonia, the sentence was carried out. Don Cristobal was hanged from the yardarm of a pinnace which was then sailed up and down the columns of the fleet as a grisly warning to those who might be inclined to disobey the Duke's commands. Captain Cuellar was not a nobleman, and it is not known why de Bobadilla should have sent him to the Auditor-General to be hanged.

Once more the angry captain clambered over the side into a pinnace and was brought to the Auditor-General. He had scarcely stepped on deck when he began a tirade against the Duke and the Major-General. His rage was white hot and it must have impressed Martin de Aranda. Cuellar maintained that the sentence was a travesty of justice and that it would forever be a stain on the honour of his family. The Auditor-General was impressed. He decided that until Bobadilla sent him an order in writing to have Captain Cuellar executed the sentence would not be carried out. No order in writing came from the Major-General. This is not surprising because he was not asked for it. Cuellar's life was spared. He remained on that ship which was the *San Juan de Sicilia*—one of the three great ships wrecked at Streeda Strand on the coast of County Sligo.

'I remained,' wrote Cuellar in his account of his adventures, 'on board this ship where we were all in great danger of death, rough weather coming on and the seams opening up so that we were deluged with water and we could not master it with the pumps.'

The plight of those on board the *San Juan de Sicilia* was shared by those thousands of sailors and soldiers in the Armada. On a day when the wind had abated, a council of the leaders was held. A number of them were in favour of sailing to Norway. There were some who wanted to sail to Ireland. The decision was left eventually to the Commander-in-Chief, and it was his decision that the fleet would sail northwards until sufficient sea room had been gained for a long starboard tack that would bring them back to Spain. Juan de Recalde, who had become ill after the battle at Gravelines, had taken to his bunk and was not present at the council.

After the decision had been taken, a man bent over a table in a cabin in the flag-ship. Before him was stretched a chart. Nobody now knows the name of this man, but if you show the plot he made to a modern navigator he will agree that the Spaniard who set the course for the return of the Armada knew his business exceedingly well. If all the commanders had followed the course he had charted, the awful tragedies off the coast of Ireland would never have happened. But no blunder was made in preparing the instructions. 'You must stay together,' they began, 'and you must steer north-north-west until the latitude of 61½ degrees is reached.' This instruction would bring the fleet north of the Shetlands, quite close to the coast of Norway. Then the ships were to sail west until they were back on the meridian of the Shetlands, whereupon they were to steer west-south-west until the fleet reached the latitude of 58 north. The nameless navigator was cautious. He avoided the dangers of the most northerly points of the Shetlands, and he provided for a clear one hundred miles of safety between the Armada and the islands off the Scottish coast. When the ships were out in the broad expanse of the Atlantic and clear of all danger, then—and only then—were they to steer south-west until they reached 53 north.

That plot would leave the Armada at least 400 miles to the west of the mouth of the river Shannon and give a safe run to many of the ports of Spain. And so they sailed until the great fleet was in latitude 58 degrees north, off Rockall. This is a small cone of granite—the most isolated speck of rock in the world it has been called—only seventy feet in height, its top snow-white from the droppings of innumerable birds that have made it their home. To reach this lonely sliver of rock the pilots steered into the Atlantic from north Uist in the Hebrides for forty

miles until the near-barren island of St. Kilda peeped
above the skyline. Another 200 miles of sailing brought
them to the cone of Rockall. It was here in this bleak
expanse of sea that some of the Spaniards made a tragic
mistake. It was a mistake made in face of the warning
of the Duke of Medina Sidonia. 'Take great care,' he had
told them, 'not to fall upon the coast of Ireland because
of the harm that may come to you there.' Some accepted
that advice. Others, to their cost, disregarded it. For that
disregard thousands of men paid in the terrible price of
their lives.

It is probable that those who disregarded the advice of
the Duke had no other choice. Juan Martinez de Recalde
was one of them. Although he was ill he still had command
of his ship. His order to make for the Irish coast must
have been prompted by knowledge of the desperate plight
in which his crew and the crews of many of the other ships
found themselves. Daily the toll of deaths had risen.
In some vessels there had been no drinking water for more
than fourteen days. Scores of soldiers and seamen died
from infected wounds, others died from thirst and virtual
starvation. Dysentery had struck in almost every ship.
In the stores the food that remained was putrid and stank
so much that no one could enter the holds. Cheese, bacon
and rice were infested with maggots and uneatable even
by men who were starving. Each cask of water opened
brought a trickle of green, slime-topped liquid. Those
who drank it rarely lived to drink again. The food-stores
were ill-ventilated and humid. Much of the supply of
provisions in each ship was stored over the sand ballast.
Through the decks seeped contaminated water. Hygiene
was unknown, especially to the soldiers on board. Hundreds
of them were given accommodation on top of the food
barrels and casks. The action of bacteria was unknown
and food was frequently stored in barrels which had been
washed in water drawn from harbours made foul by filth
of all kinds.

For seven weeks they had been at sea. Long ago they had thrown overboard many hundreds of horses and mules. Scottish fishing vessels which were keeping a wary eye on the Armada returned to their ports to tell that for miles they had sailed through hundreds of floating carcases.

It must be remembered, too, that all those on board the ships of the Armada lived in a state of squalor. Hundreds of men were crammed within their hulls. In ordinary sailing conditions a ship might have accommodation for fifty men at most. In the case of the Armada many hundreds used the same space. Knowledge of hygiene in the sixteenth century was primitive, and still less was there knowledge of the cause of sea-disease. Entire crews had died on many occasions from what may have been typhus, but which may well have been food-poisoning. Sickness had been the constant subject of reports to the Duke of Medina Sidonia by his commanders ever since the departure from Corunna. This is not surprising when the method of storage of food is taken into account. Before many days had elapsed bread would have been covered in green mould, fish would have been putrescent, cheese and rice would have become a loathsome sight with crawling maggots.

The ships themselves were in no better shape. A number of them had suffered severely from the guns of the English fleet. The shot-holes had been patched with cow-hide or with rough planking, but water poured through. On almost every vessel men who could scarcely stand—so great was their hunger and thirst—worked at the creaking pumps. While the wind clung to the west, becoming more fierce with every passing day, the ships ploughed on. Whenever they braced around to the wind, spars that had been weakened by cannon-fire give way and their rigging broke and came coiling and snaking across the decks. The *San Martin* was seriously damaged. On the water-line a great hole had been torn. This had been patched, but from widening seams the water poured into her hull.

Juan de Recalde's *San Juan de Portugal* was also taking water. Other ships were slowly sinking lower and lower as the water within them inched higher.

When the Duke took his decision to sail in a great arc around the northern tip of Ireland he had with him 110 vessels of the 128 which had sailed from Corunna. It is not known with certainty how that tight formation came to be broken. It may have been a storm or more probably a dense fog. Whatever the reason there came a morning when only 94 ships sailed in company with the flag-ship These held resolutely to their course. The second and smaller group later made contact with Juan de Recalde's *San Juan de Portugal* and these were the ships which approached the coast of Ireland. They had no other choice. Water they had to have or they would die. Repairs would have to be made before they could survive for many more days in the Atlantic. Ireland was their only hope. Dipping their yardarms in the deep swell of the ocean, the wounded ships and their starving and thirst-crazed crews approached the Irish coast.

It is significant that the ships that were in worst shape were those in the Squadron of the Levant—the ships drawn from their home ports of Genoa, Venice, Ragusa, Barcelona and from Sicily. The men who sailed them were experienced. The Mediterranean and the Adriatic could provide spectacular storms, but the Atlantic gales appear to have been too much for ships designed for trade in sunnier waters. Many of the Levanters—all converted merchant ships—were to be numbered among the wrecks on the Irish coast. Structurally the Biscayans, under Juan de Recalde, the Guipuzcoans under Miguel de Oquendo, and the Andalusians under Pedro de Valdez, were of a stouter design. The galleons of Portugal which sailed with the Armada were a mixed lot. The declining fortunes of an empire may have had an effect on the standard of shipbuilding and repair. Best of all were the galleons of proud Castile. The number of ships which gravitated to the leadership of the ailing Juan de Recalde may have been 28. This is the total of Spanish ships sighted off the Irish coast and reported to the Queen's officers. It is possible, however, that these sightings may have been made at different times and at different sections of the coast and that the reports may have been inaccurate.

Among those who sailed for Ireland there may have been many who were familiar with Irish harbours—fishermen and traders. But their knowledge extended only to the coastline of the South. So numerous were these small fishing-boats of Spain on the Irish coast in 1588 that, not long before the Armada had sailed, Francis Drake had drawn up a plan for capturing all of them. The sea off the south coast of Ireland in that distant century seemed to have been as rich in fish as are the fishing grounds off Iceland today.

The Spaniards had another advantage in sailing to Ireland. The prevailing south-westerly and north-westerly winds made the voyage to and from Spain an easy one. Yet it is now known that when the masters of the Spanish galleons and store-ships lost contact with the ship in which Juan de Recalde lay ill they became hopelessly lost, and they displayed abysmal ignorance of one of the most dangerous coastlines in Europe.

It is probable that the charts they used were grossly inaccurate. Some of the captains may have had spread before them a map of Ireland published by Mercator ten years before the Armada sailed. This was an accurate chart of the Eastern Atlantic. It would appear that not many copies of that chart were kept in the lockers of the Spanish ships. The hazy knowledge of the western seaboard of Ireland at that time is reflected in a map published in 1610 by Norden. In this example of inaccurate cartography a line drawn from Teelin Head, in Donegal, to a point off the Blaskets on the Kerry coast, represents a safe course for a ship to clear all land. In fact, the north coast of Mayo, ending in Eagle Island, projects forty miles westward of this line. In the path of these doomed ships lay the great bulge of Connacht. Despite their skill in navigation, the Spaniards were sailing into a deadly trap.

In the national archives of Spain may be seen yellowing charts which prove how experienced and skilful were these Spanish sailors. From an inspection of Armada log-books, where these have survived, their observations taken by the cross-staff or astrolabe may be shown to have been accurate.

They fixed longitude at sea by a combination of dead reckoning with latitude sights. The use of the log was unknown, and the method of Great Circle sailing was still in the future. One ship of the Armada, having obtained her latitude by observation, fixed her position by sounding in 125 fathoms on Rockall bank and entered her distance from the Irish coast as 95 leagues which was about the distance to Erris Head in Mayo.

Those Spaniards who escaped death by drowning and who were interrogated by Queen Elizabeth's representatives showed a most extraordinary ignorance of the coast on which they had foundered. Many survivors were soldiers who knew nothing of the problems which the sailors were trying to solve. But even the sailors were baffled by the tangles of the Irish coast. Many of them referred to the wreck of their ships on 'Cape Clear' which seemed to be the only landfall they knew. The Armada had been well-provided with pilots who were familiar with the coast of England and the coasts of the Netherlands and of France. But there sailed with the ships few men who had a sailorman's knowledge of the Irish coast. Juan Martinez de Recalde took precautions to remedy this lack of knowledge. He himself had been to Ireland before. He had sailed to Smerwick in 1580 with the forlorn force of Spaniards and Italians who fortified Dun an Oir—a force which was not long afterwards massacred by the English. Yet although he had this experience of sailing inshore in Irish waters, de Recalde took the precaution of seizing a Scottish fishing vessel and its entire crew as the *San Juan de Portugal* rounded the northern tip of Ireland. He took the Scots on board his galleon and put a prize-crew on board the fishing vessel. Thereafter both sailed together. The smaller vessel, de Recalde knew, would be of help in reconnoitring bays and inlets, and it is also probable that the Scots acted as pilots in reaching the anchorage which he eventually found in the Blaskets Sound.

The ships which followed in the wake of de Recalde's galleon went through another ordeal. In the first days of September they were scattered in a south-west gale.

Great green waves thudded on their decks, tore at their canvas where it had not been reefed in time, and made the task of steering almost insuperable by men who were wasted by hunger and black-tongued because of the lack of water. It was then that they became separated from the one man who could have saved them, as he himself proved by his eventual return to Spain. Without Juan de Recalde thousands of the men of the Spanish Armada were doomed. According to their position to windward, this ill-fated fleet dropped upon the Irish coast at different points between September 1 and 5, 1588. Tossing, lurching and pitching from the north-west they came, and inexorably all of them were forced inshore. Fate seemed to have destined them for this end and they could not escape. Those who were farthest out in the turmoil of the Atlantic would inevitably make their landfall in the gaunt coasts of Kerry, Clare and Galway. Those ships which were closer inshore, or to leeward, would see before them the mountainous mass of the north-west corner of Mayo and they would be forced into Sligo Bay or Donegal Bay. One of these ships was fortunate. This was a store-ship whose master, taking advantage of a brief spell of wind which enabled him to tack north-west, gained an offing and escaped. As for the rest, no more unsuitable vessels for this part of the Atlantic could be found.

The Spanish galleons had lofty castles at bow and stern.

The great weight of their guns made them unseaworthy
in the pounding seas off the Irish coast. These were the
fighting ships. They were built for war. In contrast to
merchant ships they had a keel longer in proportion to
their beam. Their lofty superstructures caused such steep
rolling that in heavy seas they needed the most expert
seamanship to keep them afloat. Usually these galleons
had two decks that ran from waist to stern. On these
decks the main armament of heavy guns was mounted.
Lighter guns were placed on the timbered castle fore and
aft. From these higher points of vantage an attacker
could send boarding parties on to the deck of an enemy
ship. But most of the ships which followed Recalde were
converted merchantmen. These normally carried heavy
guns to discourage corsairs when they were on their trading
runs.

In terse words, Fernandez Duro, the Spanish historian,
sums up the reasons why Ireland became the graveyard
of the Armada. 'They were lost,' he says, 'partly from
bad pilotage, partly from bad seamanship, but chiefly
because they were leaking like sieves, had no anchors,
their masts and rigging were shattered and their water-
casks were smashed.' He might also have added, in fairness
to the memory of his fellow-countrymen, that in the
important matter of weather conditions the Armada had
been dogged by the cruellest ill-luck.

The spring of 1588 had been remarkable for the number,
strength and duration of the storms which swept Europe.
Almost from the start the great fleet had been buffeted
by strong winds. In May torrential downpours and gales
had uprooted trees and had flooded vast areas. Thunder-
storms had swept across the Continent, freakishly followed
by hailstorms. That summer, too, rain-belts had swept
continually over the Irish countryside. Centuries of
drainage have today made the terrain of Ireland vastly
different from the time of Elizabeth the First. It is probable
that the drearily wet summer of 1588 must have resulted

in huge tracts of Midland Ireland becoming waterlogged, and with consequent delay for the traveller. Those who live on the edge of the Atlantic in Ireland are not surprised when September brings storms of terrific strength. These are the storms in which the thunder of this mighty ocean can be heard many miles inland as it surges and crashes against cliffs or exposed headlands. This is the countryside in which no shrub or bush grows straight, but is forever slanted away from the Atlantic by the pressure of the great winds. In such a spell of broken weather the ships of the Armada came close to the Irish coast and through the sea-spray they saw the massive bulwarks of mountain ranges.

While the ships were still out in the Atlantic, a man sat at a table in a room in a house in Galway. He was Edward Whyte, Clerk of Her Majesty Queen Elizabeth's Council of Connacht, and he wrote these words: 'There has blown a most extreme wind and cruel storm, the like whereof hath not been seen or heard for a long time.'

CHAPTER NINE

PANIC IN THE CASTLE

SIR WILLIAM FITZWILLIAM, Lord Deputy in Ireland, was in a panic. In his long experience of administering the affairs of the House of Tudor in Ireland this state of acute stress was not unusual. He was aged 42, a lawyer who had served as Treasurer and Chief Justice of Ireland. From 1572 to 1575 he had been Lord Deputy, and in February, 1588, he had again been appointed to that high office to succeed Sir John Perrot. His panic was, no doubt, caused by the knowledge that failure to protect the Queen's interests in this part of her realm might cost him his head. Whatever the degree of his state of panic, Sir William

Fitzwilliam resolved that at all costs he would never have
to bare his neck for the executioner's axe in the Tower of
London. This may have been the reason for the barbaric
ferocity with which he treated the Spaniards who came
ashore in Ireland. It was a case of their lives or his. In
ordering the killing-off of almost all the Spanish captives
he was merely making his own life more secure. The
reason for his panic lay in the rumours which swept Europe
after the Armada had entered the English channel. Then
came stories which told of great sea-battles in which the
English fleet had suffered great losses. Francis Drake, it
was said, had been wounded. Another report said he had
been captured, and that the ships of Elizabeth had been
scattered with blood running from their scuppers. The
foundations of the throne of England had been shaken—
it was now only a matter of time before the King of Spain's
victorious army would march on London. In the capitals
of Europe the Ambassadors of King Philip did nothing
to contradict the rumours. One of them, in fact, lit a
bonfire in the courtyard of his residence in celebration of
the 'victory'. When a courier arrived at the gates of Dublin
Castle, dismounted from his sweat-lathered horse and
handed the Lord Deputy a message which told him that
Spanish ships were off the Irish coast, Sir William Fitzwilliam had a good reason for his state of panic.

Even in London at that time it was not known for certain
that the threat to the English realm had been crushed.
True, it was known at Greenwich that the Armada had
sailed northwards, but was it not possible that it would
return to the Channel, make contact once more with the
Duke of Parma and his powerful army and sweep away
all opposition on sea and on land?

Francis Drake knew better. He was a seaman who put
his knowledge of the ways of the sea into this despatch
which he sent to his Queen: 'We left the army of Spain
so far to the northwards as they could neither recover
England nor Scotland, and within three days afterwards

we were entertained with a great storm, considering the time of year. The which storm, in many of our judgments, hath not a little annoyed the enemy's army.' Drake was quite correct, but it was an assurance which Sir William Fitzwilliam in Dublin would have been glad to receive. In the event, it was not until November that Queen Elizabeth went in public procession to St. Paul's to give public thanksgiving for deliverance from invasion by Philip's army.

The fear of the Spaniards was as real in Ireland as in England. There were stories that the Spaniards had been ordered to kill every male child in England, that one ship of the Armada carried in her hold thousands of 20-feet rope-lengths as halters for the necks of Englishmen, and that another galleon was loaded with faggots to burn them alive. The Armada, it was said also, carried whips and chains, racks and thumbscrews, branding-irons and huge knives for disembowelling—all for the purpose of killing or torturing Protestants. The propaganda was widely believed. But in Ireland there was this difference—the English feared the Spaniards, but they were more afraid of the Irish whose land they had stolen and with whom they had dealt with great cruelty. Those Spanish sails that were sighted off the north-west of Ireland brought a foreboding of retribution which could be terrible and bloody.

Lord Deputy Fitzwilliam began to spread his own rumours. Although he had only a force of 300 soldiers at his disposal, he let it be known that the Lord Admiral Howard would land at Dublin with 10,000 men. He took good care that this 'news' should become quickly known throughout Ireland.

Reporting on this stratagem which is as old as war itself, the Privy Council in London was informed by the faithful Geoffrey Fenton '. . . . . this will encourage the few dutiful subjects and abate the pride of the wicked sort, but the Lord Deputy could rather have wished that 3,000 or 4,000 men had been there already, both to have daunted the traitorous sort and to encounter the foreign enemy at his first landing.'

The messages from Ireland which told of the landing of a large force of Spaniards brought a quick reaction from the Queen herself. She ordered Sir Richard Greville to prepare an army to leave the Severn for Waterford—300 soldiers from Cornwall and Devon, and 400 from Gloucestershire and Somersetshire. The army never embarked. The steady stream of reports from the Lord Deputy in Ireland soon reassured Elizabeth that the threat to her throne was being dispelled by the cold-blooded murder of the men from Spain. The order to kill was given by the Lord Deputy in a formal commission to Sir Thomas Norris, Sir George Boucher and Sir George Carew. The language in which it was written appears quaint, but it does little to soften the dreadful direction. It read: 'Whereas the distressed fleet of the Spaniards by tempest and contrary winds, through the providence of God, have been driven upon this coast, and many of them wrecked in several places in the province of Munster, where is to be thought hath not only been much treasure cast away, now subject to the spoil of the country people, but also great store of ordnance, munitions, armours, and other goods of several kinds which ought to be preserved for and to the use of her Majesty, we authorise you to make inquiry by all good means, both by oath and otherwise, to take all the hulls of ships, stores, treasure, etc., into your hands, and to apprehend and execute all Spaniards found there, of what quality soever. Torture may be used in prosecuting this inquiry.'

This was a document which sealed the fate of many hundreds of wretched men. The directions were carried out with ruthless efficiency by those who shared in the panic of the Lord Deputy. The man who showed most enthusiasm in carrying out the terms of the commission was Sir Richard Bingham, Governor of Connacht, whose headquarters were at Athlone. It was on his orders that the city of Galway was to witness an appalling massacre of hundreds of Spaniards.

As Sir Richard Bingham studied his instructions, two ships of the Armada approached the coast of County Galway. One was the transport vessel *Falco Blanco* with 103 souls on board. She was a ship of 300 tons and her armament consisted of sixteen guns. The other was the *Concepcion* of the Biscayan squadron. She carried 225 men and she was armed with eighteen guns.

One of the factors which makes identification of the Spanish ships difficult was the practice of using the same name for a number of ships in the Armada. In the Biscayan squadron alone there were two ships named *Concepcion*, and there were, at least, six *San Juans* and two *San Juan Bautistas*.

A third ship, the name of which is unknown, followed the *Falco Blanco* and the *Concepcion*. All three were forced into Galway Bay. Here, it must be recorded, is a black chapter, for not only is it said in tradition that Irishmen brought about the shipwreck of a Spanish vessel, but that they cravenly gave up those Spaniards who had escaped death by drowning to the agents of Queen Elizabeth.

The belief that men of Spanish appearance in County Galway may be descendants of men who came ashore from the ships of the Armada and inter-married with the Irish cannot stand the test of historical examination. Almost every Spaniard who set foot on the soil of County Galway was butchered or callously hanged on the instructions of Sir Richard Bingham, who, in turn, was conforming to the edict of the Lord Deputy Fitzwilliam.

The *Falco Blanco* met her doom—if tradition is to be believed, and it is usually a reliable guide—at Barna, not far west of Galway city. When this vessel shuddered and ground her keel on the rocks, most of the soldiers and sailors on board safely reached the shore. The *Concepcion* ran ashore at Duirling na Spainneach, close to Ards Castle,

at Carna. This was within the territory of the black-
visaged Tadhg na Buile O'Flaherty, of whom it is said
that he caused the Spaniards to run aground by signals
which they thought had been made to aid them. Greed
for Spanish gold, silver, silks and wine may have been
his unholy motive.

From the sequence of dates on the Elizabethan State
Papers which deal with the Armada, it would appear that
the first Spanish ships to anchor off the Irish coast were
those which reached Kerry. The Privy Council, acting
on this information, had directed Sir William Fitzwilliam
to proceed to Munster. This order may have been motivated
by fear that, although the Desmond rising had been
suppressed by extreme measures, the landing of a strong
force of Spaniards might cause another revolt with revenge
uppermost in the hearts of the Irish. But messengers from
Sir Richard Bingham came in relays to tell that there had
been Spanish shipwrecks and Spanish landings all along
the coast of the west, the north-west and the north.

If Sir Richard Bingham was distraught by the reports
which came to him almost daily in Athlone, he could be
pardoned for his acute state of anxiety. His first reaction
was to set off on horseback for the north-west, and this
he did to reach the house of Sir Hubert McDavies at
Glinsk. While he rested a courier came from his brother,
George, who was Sheriff of Sligo, to inform him that
'three Spanish ships were distressed and cast upon the
coast of the barony of Carbury in County Sligo, near the
river Bundrowes—1,800 men drowned and seven score
as came shore were executed by myself.' That allayed
Sir Richard's state of panic to a slight degree, but less
comforting news came from Galway, from Clare, and later
still, from Limerick. On the edge of Blacksod Bay the
Spaniards had seized a castle and were strengthening its
defences.

From many districts in Connacht came the gentlemen
whose hold on their large estates depended ultimately

upon the security of the English crown. Sir Richard was
joined by Captain Aubrey Brabazon, Captain Nathaniel
Smythe, Henry Malby, George Goodman and Thomas
Dillon. Each of them brought 'a goodly companie of
foot and horse'. But Sir Richard was still apprehensive.
He despatched a messenger to Sir William Fitzwilliam,
pleading for reinforcements from Dublin. None came, for
Sir William had only a tiny force at his disposal—a fact
which he did not wish to have bruited abroad lest it should
give 'those wild Irish' the idea of fomenting another revolt.

The conscientious and precise Clerk of the Connacht
Council, Edward Whyte, recorded the next series of events:
'It was thought good,' he wrote, 'by the Governor and
Council to set forth a proclamation upon pain of death
that any man who had or kept Spaniards should bring
them in and deliver them to Robert Fowley, the Provost
Marshal. Any man who held them for more than four
hours after the proclamation to be reputed a traitor.
Whereupon, Tadhg na Buile O'Flaherty, and many others,
brought their prisoners to Galway, and for that many other
Spaniards were brought to Galway from other parts of the
province, besides those which the townsmen had taken
prisoners before the Governor despatched Robert Fowley,
Captain Nathaniel Smythe and John Byrte with warrant
and commission to put them all to the sword, saving the
noblemen or such principal gentlemen as were among
them, and afterwards to repair to O'Flaherty's country
to make earnest search for those who kept any Spaniards
in their hands and to execute them in like manner, and to
take view of the great ordnance, munitions, and other
things which were in the two ships that were lost in that
country, and to see how it might be saved for the use
of her Majesty.'

The discourse of Edward Whyte continued with the
coldly factual statement: 'Whereupon they executed 300
men at Galway.'

Even when allowance is made for the brutality of that

era, it is difficult to suppress a shudder at the picture which
those words convey to the modern reader. Those men
who were done to death had come ashore weakened by
hunger and thirst, their gait still rolling with the walk of
sailors who had been many weeks on board ship. They
were in a pitiful plight and the food and shelter they so
badly needed was given to them by at least one of the
Galway chief men. He was Sir Morrogh na dTuath
O'Flaherty who, in the words of Edward Whyte, 'used
them with more favour than the Council thought meet'.
Yet so real was the threat of the Governor's proclamation
that Sir Morrogh later handed over his captives to the
Provost Marshal.

Pitiful, too, were the men who landed near Galway
from the third and nameless ship. A party of seventy
came ashore, bringing with them a cask of wine which
they hoped to barter for food and water. They were seized,
as Edward Whyte explains, 'by the townsmen,' by which
he probably meant those townsmen who were officials of
the Queen's administration or had a vested interest in
preserving it.

Among the captives who were led through the streets
of Galway were Don Luis de Cordova, brother of a
Marquis, and his nephew, Don Gonzalo de Cordova.
These men, in the eyes of Queen Elizabeth's administrators,
were a great prize. It was common in the warfare of that
time to slaughter prisoners, but the rules also permitted
ransom. A man whose relatives could pay handsomely
for his release could count on being spared death by hanging
or by the stab of dagger or sword. Don Luis was examined
and admitted he had been in charge of one hundred men
on the *Falco Blanco* and he added that his brother, the
Marquis, had an income of one thousand ducats a year.
This information was carefully noted and it certainly
saved his life and that of his nephew.

The horror of that scene of butchery in Galway when
more than 300 men were slaughtered in animal-like fashion

is best forgotten. The citizens of Galway were aghast at this callous and appalling massacre. The women of the city showed their grief by making shrouds for the bodies, and wherever they could the menfolk gave them a Christian burial. Where those graves are no one knows today, but somewhere near Galway, or perhaps under some of its modern buildings, rests the dust of the men of Spain.

In the tales of the seanachies of Galway, one may still hear of how only two men and a boy escaped death of all those who had been shipwrecked in the *Falco Blanco,* the *Concepcion,* and those who came ashore from the nameless ship. They were sheltered by the people of Galway—at great risk to their own lives—fed and clothed in many homes. Did they ever get back to Spain? Did they remain in Galway, learning to speak and to dress as Irishmen did? These are intriguing questions, but to them it is doubtful if there will ever be an answer.

In the last week of September, Sir Richard Bingham rode from Athlone to Galway, having by this time collected a strong band of foot soldiers and horsemen. Edward Whyte was again meticulously careful in recording the doings of the Governor. He reported to the Privy Council in London: 'At three o'clock in the afternoon he called Don Luis de Cordova before him and all the rest of the prisoners which were not put to the sword before, to the number of forty persons, which he commanded to be executed, saving ten of the best of them whom he committed to the custody of divers gentlemen till the Lord Deputy should have resolved what to do with them. Having made a clear dispatch of them, both within the town and the county, he rested Sunday all day, giving thanks to Almighty God for her Majesty's most happy success in that action and our deliverance from such dangerous enemies. Upon Monday morning he departed from the town of Galway, and having left all things in good order, both within the town and in every place where he travelled,

he dismissed such gentlemen and others who attended
him and so came to Athlone.'

The man who shed the blood of his wretched captives
so pitilessly was a soldier-of-fortune, a big man physically
who, at this time, was aged 62. Sir Richard Bingham
knew the Spaniards well. He had served with their army
at St. Quentin in France and he had fought side by side
with them in the great trial of strength at Lepanto against
the Turks in 1572. Then, as a volunteer, he had fought
against the Spaniards in the Low Countries on the side
of the Dutch. In 1579 he served in Ireland against Desmond,
and in 1580 he was captain of the war-vessel *Swiftsure*
under Wynter when two guns were landed from the ship
to pound the defences of the fort at Smerwick in Kerry.
This was a siege which has never been erased from the
memory of the Irish people. James Fitzmaurice had left
Ireland for Spain in an effort to enlist the aid of King
Philip. The King, however, refused the request of the
Irishman to send a strong force to Ireland, but he raised
no objection when Fitzmaurice, with the help of money
from the Archbishop of Compostella, was enabled to set
out from Spain with four small vessels and sixty Italian
and Spanish troops. The little force landed at Dingle in
July, 1579, and Fitzmaurice called on the princes and
people of Ireland to rally to his standard. The tiny force
began to fortify themselves in Dun an Oir, the Golden
Fort, situated on a promontory overlooking Smerwick
harbour. Fitzmaurice moved out to seek reinforcements
but was killed in a skirmish with the family of the Burkes—
themselves descendants of Norman invaders. Over a year
later—in September, 1580, a force of 600 Spaniards and
Italians arrived at Smerwick under the command of
Bastiano di San Giuseppi, a self-styled colonel who had
raised these volunteers on his own initiative. The defenders
of the Golden Fort were no match for the strong force
which the then Lord Deputy, Grey de Wilton, brought
to the siege. Fighting went on for some days until the

garrison surrendered on terms, but were massacred without pity on November 10. Four years afterwards Sir Richard Bingham was knighted by Sir John Perrot, who was then Lord Deputy, and appointed Governor of Connacht, an office which he held with little interruption until his death in 1599. He was a man from whom no Irishman or Spaniard could expect a scintilla of mercy.

There is another sad episode in this story. When the executions had been carried out and after a few weeks had elapsed, seven or eight other survivors of the wrecks were captured. Two of these were minor noblemen. The others were mere boys, youngsters on the threshold of manhood whose duties on the ships would have been the cleaning of cabins and the serving of food. These fell into the hands of George Bingham, brother of Sir Richard. To his credit it must be recorded that he did not imitate the brutal actions of the Governor. He spared their lives. Yet they, too, were to die. Months afterwards when Lord Deputy Fitzwilliam was making an inspection of lands held in fief to the crown, he came to Galway where he was informed that some of the hated Spaniards still survived. He ordered the execution of all of them. The two minor noblemen and the six boys (who were, in fact, Dutch and not Spaniards at all) died on the blood-stained swords of the soldiers who acted on the orders of a man who seemed to have been without a vestige of the virtue of mercy. And then, his blood-lust unsatiated, Lord Deputy Fitzwilliam ordered the execution of all the noblemen who had been removed to Athlone from Galway.

Only the lives of Don Luis de Cordova and his nephew were spared. After long negotiation a large ransom was paid by their relatives in Spain and both were returned to their homeland.

The names of those Spaniards who were executed at Athlone speak in themselves of their nobility, of their haughty pride and of their unbending military caste. They may be read in the Elizabethan State Papers, written in

ink that is brown with the passage of centuries and in a
script that is a sore trial to the eyes of the present-day
reader. There were no fewer than thirteen Dons. Among
them were Don Alonso de Argotta, Don Antonio de
Ulloa, Don Diego de Cordova, Don Diego de Santillana,
Don Alonso Ladron de Guerva and Don Diego Mieres.
With them died Pedro de Archega, captain of the *Falco
Blanco* and captain Diego Sarmiento of the *Concepcion*.

If one may read between the lines of the script in the
State Papers there developed an anxiety in the mind of
Sir Richard Bingham to put the blame for the execution
of the Spanish noblemen squarely on the shoulders of
Lord Deputy Fitzwilliam. A greedy note runs through
all the directives and orders of the period—no doubt
prompted by Walsingham, Secretary of State, who sat at
the epicentre of Elizabethan power, or by Lord Burghley
to whom great power and wealth seemed the most desirable
acquisitions. The ransom paid for the safe return of Don
Luis de Cordova and of his nephew, Don Gonzalo, must
have prompted the question: Why were the other noble
Spanish captives so wantonly slaughtered when similar
sums could have been gathered into the Queen's exchequer
by careful negotiation with their kinsmen in Spain?

To exculpate himself, Sir Richard Bingham seems to
have thought that he should send an explanation to London.
It would appear to be significant that he wrote directly
to the Queen. 'The loss to the Spaniards on the shores of
Connacht was twelve ships,' he explained. Then he continued: 'The men of these ships all perished, save 1,100
or more who were put to the sword, amongst whom were
officers and gentlemen of quality to the number of fifty,
and whose names have been set down in a list. The gentlemen were spared until the Lord Deputy sent me special
direction to see them executed—reserving alone de Cordova
and his nephew. My brother, George, had two gentlemen
and some five or six boys and young men, who, coming
after the heat of fury and justice was past, by entreaty,

I spared them, and did dispose them unto several Englishmen's hands upon good assurance that they would be forth-
coming at all times. But the Lord Deputy Fitzwilliam
came to Connacht and ordered all killed except de Cordova
and his nephew who were at Athlone.'

Sir Richard also sent to London a copy of the sailing
orders of the Armada which was found on the person of
one of the executed captains. They read—and for those
who may wish to plot the course on a modern chart they
may be of interest: 'The course that is first to be held is
to the north/north-east until you be found under 61
degrees and a half; and then to take great heed lest you
fall upon the Island of Ireland for fear of the harm that
may happen unto you upon that coast. Then, parting
from those islands and doubling the Cape in 61 degrees
and a half, you shall run west/south-west until you be
found under 58 degrees; and from thence to the south-
west to the height of 53 degrees; and then to the south/
south-west, making to the Cape Finisterre, and so to
procure your entrance into the Groin (Corunna) or to
Ferrol.'

CHAPTER TEN

CHIEFTAINS WITH MERCY

CAPTAIN FRANCISCO CUELLAR stood at the taffrail of the
converted merchantman, *San Juan de Sicilia,* and looked
at the single anchor-cable that held the ship a mile distant
from Streeda strand on the shoreline of County Sligo.
His experience of the sea told him that the anchorage was
perilous. It was trebly so with that single anchor. More
than ever he regretted the action of panic at Calais when
scores of Armada anchors were left near the French coast
as the fire-ships of the English bore down on the fleet.
This regret was to be shared by the seamen of the Armada

who sailed along the Irish coast, for those missing anchors meant the difference between life and death. More than ever, too, he regretted that his reprieve from the death sentence of Major-General de Bobadilla by his friend Martin de Aranda, the Auditor-General of the Armada, should have brought him on board the *San Juan de Sicilia*. The vessel was one of the squadron of the Levant, a squadron which proved to be alarmingly unseaworthy in the strength of Atlantic storms. They may have been old ships or they may have been built with less skill than other vessels in the fleet. But whatever may have been the reason, the ships of the Levant seemed to have had an excessive weight and height in their masts. The leverage of this mistake in design caused a strain on the hulls which necessitated the constant employment of caulkers.

When the ships that had obeyed the order of the Duke of Medina Sidonia to keep clear of the Irish coast returned to Spain it was found that six of the Biscayan squadron and ten galleons of the India Guard had made a safe passage home. Soon they were joined by seven of the ten galleons of the squadron of Portugal and eight great ships of the squadron of Andalusia. Only two of the ten big vessels of the squadron of the Levant returned. One of them was the *Regazzona*. She sailed home with 400 on board—but of the total number of about 4,000 who sailed in these Levantine ships, 3,527 died from disease, in battle, by drowning or by execution in Ireland.

The *Regazzona* had an advantage in size over the other ships in the squadron of the Levant. She was well over 1,000 tons and she was commanded by Don Martin de Bertendona, a man who was wise by tradition and training in the ways of the sea. His father had also followed the sea and had, in fact, been chosen as captain of the ship which had brought King Philip to England, in July 1554, to marry Henry VIII's eldest daughter, Mary Tudor.

Less fortunate than those who sailed with Don Martin de Bertendona were the 307 men who were on board the

600-tonner, *Santa Maria de Vision,* the complement of 395 men on the 860-ton *Juliana,* the 274 men who perished in the 728-ton *Lavia,* and the transport-ship *Santiago.* These four Levanters cannot be clearly identified with unnamed wrecks on the Irish coast, but it seems probable that all four were lost between Broadhaven and the Rosses of County Donegal. There are records which show that, in 1596, survivors from the *Lavia* and the *Juliana* were still in Ireland. Two names in a list of prisoners, Manuel Orlando and Vicenzio Debartulo, both described as Venetian captains, seem to be those of the masters of the *Lavia* and the *Santa Maria de Vision.*

Captain Cuellar did not, of course, know the extent of the disaster which had befallen the other ships of the Squadron of the Levant. Later he was to record: 'The vessel on which I sailed was from the Levant and had for consort two very large vessels, we keeping together so as to be able to give mutual aid.' The record of his shipwreck, his subsequent adventures in Ireland, and the story of his escape to the Continent are preserved in a letter which he wrote from Antwerp in October, 1589, to a friend in Spain. It had been preserved for three centuries in the archives of the *Academia de la Historia* in Madrid and was discovered by the Spanish historian, Captain Cesareo Fernandez Duro, towards the end of the last century. All three of the vessels to which he refers were wrecked on or near Streeda strand.

For four days the great ships had strained at their anchors at that point of the coast which is dominated by the squat bulk of Benbulben mountain. 'On the fifth day,' wrote Captain Cuellar, 'there came a great tempest which took us on the quarter, with a sea running as high as Heaven, so that neither could our hawsers stand the strain nor could the sails be of any service. The ships were driven ashore on a beach of fine sand, and in the space of an hour the three vessels went to pieces. Of their crews, not more than 300 escaped, while more than 1,000 were drowned, among them being many noblemen, chief officers, gentlemen, and other persons and all their suites.

'Don Diego Enriquez, the hunchback Major-General, met his death in a most miserable manner. Frightened by the heavy seas which were running and which passed clear over the ships, he took to a small boat which had a deck. Along with him went the son of the Count of Villafranca and two other Portuguese gentlemen, having on their persons jewels and coin to the value of 16,000 ducats. Having stowed themselves beneath the deck, they ordered the hatch to be closed and caulked. As they were casting off, more than seventy desperate sailors and soldiers threw themselves into the boat. At that moment the small boat was struck by an immense wave which completely covered it and carried away all these people, and then the boat went whirling about in the heavy sea until it was cast ashore, keel upwards and in such a condition that the gentlemen who were within the small shelter deck beneath the hatch died there.

'Then came along some savages who turned the boat over in order to strip it of iron fittings and nails. Breaking open the hatch, they took out the dead bodies and stripped them, taking all the money and jewels that they found on them, and after that they threw the bodies aside without any attempt whatsoever at burial. From the stern of the ship I looked at the pitiful scene that lay before me, many being drowned in the vessel, others throwing themselves into the raging sea and sinking without again coming to the surface, others calling aloud for help and imploring God's aid.

'I knew not what to do, not knowing how to swim and the waves being great. On land there was the shore lined with enemies who were dancing and jumping around with joy at the sight of our misfortune, and when anyone of our people reached the shore, down on him they came and at once stripped him of every stitch he had on him and then ill-treated him and left him covered with wounds.

'I went to the aid of Martin de Aranda (the Auditor-General of the Armada who had spared his life), and I found him very woebegone and miserable. I asked him what he wished to do to save his life before the vessel had finished breaking up, saying that she would not hold together more than a quarter of an hour, as, in truth, she did not. Already the greater part of the crew, as well as the captain and officers, had been either drowned or killed when I resolved on making an effort to save my life. I therefore got on a hatch or a piece of the hull which had been broken off and Martin de Aranda followed me, loaded as he was with escudos which he carried sewn up in his doublet and hose. The piece of wreckage, however, would not come away from the hull, being bound to it by heavy chains, while the heavy seas and much floating timber beat so against it as to cause us great pain. I sought out, therefore, some other mode of rescue which was to throw myself on a hatch about the size of a table, which seemingly by the mercy of God, had been brought within my reach. I sought to get on it, but down I went some six good fathoms and took in so much water that I was almost drowned. Coming again to the surface, I called to Martin de Aranda and was able to get him on to the hatch with me.

'As we cleared ourselves of the ship and were getting away from her, there came an immense wave which struck us with such force that Martin de Aranda, not being able to hold on, was swept away and was drowned, crying aloud for help, and calling on God as he disappeared. It was now out of my power to aid him since the hatch, being now unloaded at one extremity, started to turn over with me, while at the very same moment a piece of floating timber almost broke my legs.

'I, therefore, with great resolve, got firmly fixed on the hatch, calling for help to Our Lady of Ontanar. Just then there came in quick succession four waves, and without knowing how, and unable as I was to swim, I was carried to land where I got out of the water unable to stand up and covered with blood, wounds and bruises.'

That was how Captain Francisco Cuellar came to Ireland. He was fortunate to have been washed ashore at a place where he was able to crawl unobserved and to hide in a clump of rushes. Bloodstained and exhausted, his breath coming in quick, panting gasps, he was soon overcome by a welcome oblivion. He regained consciousness to find that he had been joined in the shelter of the rushes by a young man who had been stripped completely naked and who was in such a state of extreme shock that he could not speak. Dusk was creeping over the desolation of the seashore, the wind was blowing with decreasing force and the sea crashed with a lessening thunder on the strand.

Tormented by pain, hunger and thirst, Captain Cuellar thought his last moments had come when out of the grey gloom there came the tall figures of two men, one of whom carried a spear, the other a great iron axe. Slowly the two approached the prostrate castaways. Then, when Cuellar expected to find the searing pain of a spear thrust through his body or to feel the thud of the axe as it crushed his skull, the tall men pulled armfuls of rushes which they piled over the Spanish captain and his still-dumb companion. That done, and without speaking a single word, the man with the spear and the man with the axe went to the shore to rip open boxes and to take away anything they could carry from the wrecks.

Captain Cuellar fell into a sleep of sheer exhaustion. It was dark when he was awakened by the sound of about 200 horsemen who were making their way to share in the loot from the ships. He turned around to speak to his companion, but the young man who had been so terror-struck that he had been bereft of speech, was dead. Once more Captain Cuellar fell asleep. When he awoke, dawn had come. The body of his companion was grotesquely stiffened in death. In Spain, in Portugal or in Italy a mother would grieve for a son who would never return.

Captain Cuellar crawled to a point from which he could see the beach. From his hiding place the sight which met his eyes was, indeed, horrifying. 'I saw,' he wrote, 'more than 800 corpses which the sea had thrown up on the shore. The ravens and the wild dogs fed on them without anyone being there to give them burial—not even to poor Don Diego Enriquez.'

With great caution he moved away from the scene of the wreckage until he came upon a small church which had recently been burned. It was, without much doubt, the abbey of Staad, a few of the stones of which may still be seen today, moss-grown and weathered by the passage of the centuries. Tradition says that the little church— no more than 34 feet in length and 14 feet wide—was founded by St. Molaise, patron saint of the island of Inishmurray which is close to the mainland at that point. Until the last islander moved to the mainland a few years ago it was customary to light beacons for the purpose of answering signal-fires on the island, signals which meant that the services of a priest or doctor were urgently required by the islanders. The mainlanders throughout the centuries invariably lit their fire outside the wall of the church.

It was within this church on a grey September day that Captain Cuellar saw a gruesome sight. From the iron bars which were fitted into the windows swung the bodies of twelve of his countrymen, their necks twisted in the grip of the noose with which each of them had been hanged. He described it thus: 'I went to the church which was forsaken, the images of the saints burned and destroyed, and within were twelve Spaniards hanged by the English Lutherans who were prowling around in quest of us in order to finish with all who had escaped from the disasters of the sea. All the friars had fled to the mountains through fear of these enemies who would have killed them had they caught them, leaving neither church nor friary standing and making them watering-places for cows and pigs.' There was silence within the church, the silence that comes

after terrible deeds. Captain Cuellar moved away from
the terrible sight in that little church which was never to
be rebuilt.

Becoming weaker with every hour that passed, Captain
Cuellar found a path which led through a thick wood.
He followed the path for about a mile until he suddenly
came upon a very old woman who was driving five or six
cows to a hiding-place within the wood. By signs the
woman warned him not to go farther along the path.
Disconsolately he turned back the way he had come until
he was once more near the shore where many groups of
people were moving to and fro, carrying away all the
wreckage of the ships. He dared not approach them for
fear that they would strip him of the few clothes he wore
or even kill him. Then quite suddenly he saw two Spanish
soldiers running towards him. Both were as naked as the
day they were born. One of them had a severe head
wound. Captain Cuellar called to them from his hiding-
place. They came to him and told him how the English
soldiers had cruelly done to death more than a hundred
Spaniards who had fallen into their hands. The three
were so weak with hunger that they would take any risk
to obtain a morsel of food. They decided to move down
to a section of the beach which was deserted in the hope
of finding some kind of foodstuff that might have been
washed in from the wrecked ships.

'We began to see bodies, most miserable and pitiful to
look upon, as the sea threw them up from time to time on
the strand so that in that place there were more than 400,'
Captain Cuellar recorded. He continued with his narrative:
'Some of them we recognised, among them poor Don
Diego Enriquez whose body, even in the midst of my
distress, I could not bring myself to pass without burying
it in a hole which we made in the sand at the water's edge.
Along with him we buried another captain much honoured
and my great friend. Hardly had we covered them when
there came down to us 20 savages to see what we were

about. We gave them to understand by signs that we had
buried there these men who were our brothers in order
that their bodies might not become food for the ravens.
We separated from them in search of food along the beach,
such as the biscuits which the waves were washing up.

'Just then four savages came upon us and began to take
the little clothing I wore, but another of them who seemed
to be a leader pushed them aside and ordered them to leave
me alone. This leader put us on a road which led from the
shore to a village where he lived. There was for me the
further misery that the road was very rough with big stones
so that without pain I could not put one foot beyond the
other, being in my bare feet and suffering agony as well
in one leg in which there was a wound. My poor companions, who were entirely naked and frozen with cold,
then very sharp, were more dead than alive and could not
render me any assistance. They went ahead, and, little
by little, I reached the top of a hill where I discovered
some thatched huts.'

But before he reached the little village, Captain Cuellar
had to traverse a wood. He had scarcely entered it when
he met two young men who were accompanied by an old
man and a girl who was about twenty years of age. They
were, Cuellar thought, on their way to the shore in search
of plunder. The two young men attacked him savagely.
One of them thrust at him with a knife. The Spanish
captain, weakened as he undoubtedly was by his privations,
parried the blow with a stick which he carried, but the
knife-point wounded him in a leg. The intervention of the
old man and the girl saved his life. The young men tore
off his clothing, finding as they did so a gold chain worth
more than a thousand ducats. When the young men
made this find they were delighted and rummaged through
his doublet and hose thread by thread. In the doublet
they found 45 gold crowns which had been given to him at
Corunna as two months' pay. The girl was grieved to see
him treated so and entreated the young men to return the

clothes. This they did, and Cuellar donned the clothing which had been rent and torn. The old man and the young men went away, but the girl remained. Among the belongings of which he had been robbed were some relics contained in a small locket. The girl had been handed the locket and a slender silver chain. These she hung around her neck, making signs that she wished to keep the relics and the locket which was marked with the insignia of the Brotherhood of the Holy Trinity.

Captain Cuellar was more fortunate than his companions. The girl left him and shortly afterwards a boy came towards him bringing with him a poultice of herbs which he placed on the Spaniard's wounds. He went away to return with milk, butter and oaten bread. Captain Cuellar drank the milk and ate the bread with ravenous haste and immediately began to feel stronger. The boy signalled to him to follow a road which ran close to the village, but warned him by signs that he was not to approach the huts.

Limping along with the aid of a stout stick, Captain Cuellar survived on a diet of berries and watercress. But his privations were not at an end. Once more he was set upon by a group of men who beat him mercilessly and stripped him of every one of his tattered garments. To cover his nakedness he plaited ferns and rushes into a primitive form of skirt. Journeying on he came to a lake to find a cluster of huts at the edge of the water. This little village appeared to be deserted, but sheltering within the thatched hovels he found three other Spaniards who had escaped from the beach. Thankful that at least he had some of his fellow-countrymen to share his hardship and misery, Captain Cuellar fell asleep on the straw-covered floor of one of the huts. How long he and his companions stayed by the lakeside Captain Cuellar does not say, but an encounter with a young man who spoke a little Latin gave them hope of improving their lot. The young man told them that six leagues distant from the lake there lay a friendly country that belonged to a great lord who was a good friend to the King of Spain. The great chieftain had harboured all the Spaniards who had come to him.

The Spaniards followed the directions given to them by the young man and Captain Cuellar was able to record:

'God was pleased to bring us to a land of some safety where we found a village belonging to better people, Christian and kindly. In that village there were seventy Spaniards and the women and children cared for them most charitably. The chief was not there at this time.

'Although he is a savage, he is a very good Christian and an enemy of the heretics and always fights against them. His name is Lord de Ruerge.'

Captain Cuellar had reached a village which was within the territory of Brian O'Rourke of Breffni, a man who was later to pay with his life for the hospitality he had shown to the castaway Spaniards. Having rested at the village for a number of days, Captain Cuellar, now dressed in a cloak and trousers which were covered with lice, set off with his fellow-Spaniards northwards to reach a Spanish ship which had sheltered in a harbour to make repairs. They had not gone far when news came to them that the ship had sailed. Disappointed, the little group of castaways returned to the country of O'Rourke where the chieftain sheltered, fed and clothed them. Captain Cuellar, in the account of his adventures and tribulations has left an interesting word-picture of the people with whom he spent this period of exile.

'The Chieftain's wife,' he wrote, 'was exceedingly comely. I told her and the other womenfolk their fortunes as they sat in the sun. I told them a hundred thousand nonsensical things at which they were mightily pleased. But day and night both men and women followed me incessantly, asking me to have their fortunes told. The nature of these savages is to live like beasts among the mountains, some of which are very rugged in this part of the island where

we were cast away. They live in huts made of straw. The
men have big bodies, their features and limbs are well-
made, and they are as agile as deer. They eat but one meal
a day and that at night, and their ordinary food is bread
of an oaten kind and butter. They drink sour milk as
they have no other beverage, but no water, although it
is the best in the world. On feast-days they eat meat,
half-cooked, without bread or salt. They dress in tight
breeches and goatskin jackets cut short but very big. Over
all they wear a blanket or cloak and they wear their hair
down to their eyes. They are good walkers and have great
endurance.

'They are always at war with the English who garrison
the country, and both defend themselves from them and
prevent them from coming into their territory which is
all flooded and covered with marshy ponds. Their great
bent is to be robbers and to steal from one another, so that
not a day passes without a call to arms among them.
For when the men of one village learn that there are cattle
or anything else in another village, they go at once armed
at night and shouting war-cries to kill one another. When
the English learn which village has gathered in the most
cattle, they swoop down on it and take all way. These
people have no other help than to fly to the mountains
with their wives and flocks, for they possess no other
property, neither household staff nor clothes. They sleep
on the ground upon rushes freshly cut and full of water
or else frozen stiff. Most of the women are pretty but
ill-dressed. They wear nothing but a shift and a cloak over
it, and a linen cloth much-folded on their heads and tied
in front. They are hard workers and good housewives
after their fashion. These people call themselves Christians,
hear Mass and follow the usages of the Church. Almost
all their churches, monasteries and hermitages have been
destroyed by the soldiers from the English garrisons and
by their own countrymen who have joined them, for they
are as bad as the English. In this country there is neither

justice nor right, and everybody does what he likes. These
savages liked us very much for they knew that we were
great enemies to the heretics and had come to fight them.
Had it not been for these people not one of us would now
be alive. These savages got a great quantity of jewels
and money from us and from those ships of our fleet that
were cast ashore, for there were many people of great
possessions on board who were all drowned.'

Captain Cuellar, moving from the territory of O'Rourke,
was given shelter, with his companions, by the Chieftain
MacClancy in his stronghold castle. From the topo-
graphical detail which Captain Cuellar gives it would
appear that the castle was that which is now a ruin on the
southern shore of Lough Melvin, some distance to the
westward of the island of Inisheher.

There can be no certainty about this. The castle may
have been on the north-east side of Lower Lough Erne,
or possibly on the south-west side, opposite Derrygonnelly.
But the Cuellar narrative fits most closely the Rosclogher
site.

'The name of the Chieftain with whom I lived,' Captain
Cuellar explained, 'was Manglana. This Chieftain was
always a great enemy of the Queen and never loved anything that was hers, nor would he obey her, and therefore
the English Governor of this part of the island wanted
very much to take him prisoner.'

A decision of the English to march into MacClancy's
territory may have been prompted by rumours of a large
force of Spaniards who were mustering around this chieftain
who had so far resisted all appeals to submit to Elizabeth's
rule. Not long after Captain Cuellar had been welcomed
by MacClancy, news came that a strong force of soldiers
was advancing northwards. The time was November.

Captain Cuellar continues his story: 'When the Chieftain
heard of the great force of 1,700 men that was coming
against him, knowing he had no means of resistance, he
resolved to fly to the mountains, which, in default of an

army, were his only means of safety. We Spaniards who were with him already had news of the evil that was coming upon us, and we did not know what to do nor where to turn for safety. One Sunday after Mass, the Chieftain, blazing with anger, his hair hanging down over his eyes, took us apart and said he could not entertain any hope of defence and that he had made up his mind to fly with all his people, their flocks and families, and we must look to what we should do to save ourselves. I made answer that if he would wait for a little while we would give him a reply. I withdrew apart with the eight Spaniards that were with me—they were brave companions—and said to them it was better to die with honour rather than to wander as fugitives over the mountains naked and barefoot in the freezing cold. We should, I said, defend the Chieftain's castle to the death. This we could well do against twice as strong a force as that which was coming against us.'

In his letter to his friend, the former captain of the *San Pedro* described MacClancy's stronghold. The castle was, he said, strongly constructed and it would be difficult to capture unless the attacker used artillery. It was built, he explained, on the shore of a deep lake which was more than a league wide. The outlet to the sea was tidal, but even at low tide the security of the stronghold was not affected. He considered that it was well-nigh impregnable, both by water and by the strip of land by which it was approached. For a league around the village—which was built on solid ground—there was a marsh into which a man could sink chest-high, and the village could be reached only by the use of certain paths.

'The Chieftain was pleased at our resolve,' wrote Captain Cuellar who then continued with his story: 'In order that we should not play him false, the Chieftain made us take an oath that we would not abandon his castle nor surrender it to an enemy, upon any terms or conditions and although we should starve to death, and that we would not open the gates to let in any Englishman, Irishman or Spaniard, or anyone at all, until the Chieftain should return in person. After all the necessary things had been done, we put the ornaments from the church into the castle and some relics that were there. We also laid in three or four boat-loads of stones, half a dozen muskets, a half-a-dozen arquebuses and some other weapons. The Chieftain embraced us and then betook himself to the mountains whither his people had already gone.'

The force which marched in the name of Queen Elizabeth into MacClancy's territory was, in all probability, led by George Bingham, the Sheriff of Sligo and a brother of Sir Richard Bingham, the Governor of Connacht, who had dealt so mercilessly with the Spanish captives at Galway. The action of Brian O'Rourke and of MacClancy in giving refuge to Spaniards was well-known to the English. One of many reports read: 'Certain Spaniards, being stripped, were relieved by O'Rourke, apparelled, and new furnished with weapons.'

Supporting this probability is the record of a plaintive message from George, the Sheriff, to his brother which stated that in his absence from Sligo his stables and three horses were burned by the O'Connors, the O'Harts and the O'Dowds, 'who', the Sheriff said, 'call themselves King Philip's men'.

Captain Cuellar described the arrival of the English force at the castle. His eye for defensive terrain was expert. The would-be attackers could not get close enough to mount an attack because of the boggy nature of the ground. From a distance the English commander shouted threats. When these did not appear to have any effect on the defenders he promised that if they surrendered they would get safe conduct back to Spain. That promise received no consideration from Captain Cuellar who relates that the English hanged two Spaniards in full view of their country-men in the castle, hoping, no doubt, that the terror of this action would have more effect than threats or promises. The siege continued for seventeen days, and at the end

of that period Captain Cuellar was able to write: 'God
was pleased to help us and to deliver us from our enemies
by means of terrible storms and heavy snows that came
upon them in such manner that they were forced to raise
the siege and to march away.'

When MacClancy returned to his castle he gave Captain
Cuellar and his companions many presents and from the
other chief men of the territory came other gifts. MacClancy
was so delighted with the outcome of the defence of his
castle, and so anxious that these gallant Spaniards should
remain with him, that he offered the hand of his sister in
marriage to Captain Cuellar. This offer was declined with
as much delicacy as the circumstances permitted. The
captain told the chieftain that if he wished to show his
appreciation he could provide him with guides to conduct
him northwards where a ship might be found to take him
to Scotland. MacClancy countered this suggestion by
saying that the paths were then not safe. To remove himself
from this embarrassing situation Captain Cuellar resolved
to leave the MacClancy country secretly. This he did with
four Spanish comrades ten days after Christmas. Together
they marched towards the north where the writ of the
Queen had less power. Their search became more purpose-
ful when they learned of a bishop who had arranged
an escape-route for a number of other Spaniards. Captain
Cuellar does not record the name of the bishop, but there
can be little doubt that it was the Bishop of Derry, Redmond
O'Gallagher, believed to have been one of the three Irish
bishops who attended sessions of the Council of Trent.

'I travelled in search of this bishop who lived in a castle
whither he had fled to seek refuge from the English,' Captain
Cuellar wrote. 'This bishop was a very good Christian.
He went about dressed as a savage in order not to be
discovered, and I could not hold back my tears when I
went up to him and kissed his ring. He had twelve Spaniards
with him, meaning to help them cross to Scotland, and he
was greatly pleased at my coming, especially when he

learned that I was a sea-captain. I stayed six days with
this bishop who showed me great hospitality and who
arranged for a pinnace to take us all to Scotland, a journey
which usually took two days. The bishop gave us supplies
and said Mass for us in the castle. May God keep him
in His protection and deliver him from his enemies! I
put to sea in the pinnace in which there were eighteen of
us. That same day the wind was contrary and we were
obliged to run before it in the direction of the Hebrides
where we reached land in the morning—our boat almost
full of water and the mainsail torn. From there, after two
days of good weather, we began our voyage to Scotland
which we reached in three days—not without danger
because the boat took in so much water.'

Captain Cuellar did not seem to have been happy in his
sojourn in Scotland where he stayed for six months. His
hopes, and the hopes of other Spaniards who had landed
from Armada ships on the Scottish coast, were centred
in the effort which the Duke of Parma was making to have
them repatriated. At last news came that the Duke had
arranged for a Scotsman who owned four small vessels
at a Flanders port to sail to Scotland and to return with
the remnant of the Armada force. The cost would be four
ducats a head.

The plan was not kept secret. Soon after the four small
vessels had sailed, the Dutch sent heavily armed ships to
await their return. For six weeks they kept this vengeful
vigil. When the four vessels with the returning Spaniards
on board came close to shore they were attacked by the
Dutchmen. Two of the smaller vessels were captured
immediately and everyone on board was slain. Two ships
ran aground and many of those on board were drowned.
Captain Cuellar was shipwrecked once more. Clutching
at a baulk of timber he propelled himself ashore.

'I got to land with nothing but my shirt,' he wrote,
'and it was pitiful to see us enter the city of Dunkirk so
naked. Looking out to sea we saw under our very eyes

the Dutch killing more than two hundred Spaniards—not leaving three alive.'

So ended the adventures and the letter of Captain Francisco Cuellar. What was the fate of the men who had befriended him in Ireland? The O'Rourke of Breffni shortly afterwards fled to Scotland where he was arrested. He was brought to London, arraigned on a charge of high treason, found guilty and hanged.

It was that trial and sentence which gave T. D. Sullivan inspiration for his verses: 'O'Rourke's Request':

> On that wild day when near our coast
>   the stately ships of Spain,
> Caught in a fierce and sudden storm,
>   for safety sought in vain,
> When, wrenched and torn 'midst mountain waves,
>   some foundered in the deep,
> And others broken on sunken reefs
>   and headlands rough and steep.
>
> I heard the cry that, off my land
>   where breakers rise and roar,
> The sailors from a sinking ship
>   were striving for the shore.
> I hurried to the frightful scene,
>   my generous people, too —
> Men, women, even children came
>   some kindly deed to do.
>
> We saw them clutching spars and planks
>   that soon were washed away,
> Saw others bleeding on the rocks,
>   low moaning where they lay;
> Some cast ashore and back again,
>   dragged by the refluent wave,
> Whom one grip from a friendly hand
>   would have sufficed to save.

We rushed into the raging surf,
  watched every chance, and when,
They rose and rolled within our reach,
  we grasped the drowning men.
We took them to our hearts and homes,
  and bade them there remain,
Till they might leave with hopes to reach
  their native land again.

This is the 'treason' you have charged!
  Well, treason let it be,
One word of sorrow for such fault
  you'll never hear from me.
I'll only say, although you hate
  my race and creed and name,
Were your folk in that dreadful plight
  I should have done the same.

The Chieftain MacClancy also paid dearly for having befriended Captain Cuellar and the other Spaniards. In April, 1590, George Bingham's forces went once more into that mountainous and marshy country. This time their approach must have been more surreptitious. MacClancy, caught unaware, tried to escape by running for the lough across which he hoped to swim. A shot from a musket broke his arm and he was brought to the shore by a gallowglass. English justice was administered forthwith. MacClancy was beheaded and his head was brought to Sligo. To London was sent this report: 'He was a most barbarous creature; his country extended from Grange to Ballyshannon; he was O'Rourke's right hand; he had fourteen Spaniards with him, some of whom were taken alive.'

Captain Cuellar, without doubt, was fortunate in having decided to turn down the hand in marriage of MacClancy's sister and to have met the Bishop of Derry on the first stage of his long journey back to Spain.

A little under a century ago, a great storm shifted some of the tall sand dunes that line the Grange-Cliffoney-Mullaghmore coastline. There, revealed by the wind, were the bones of scores of men who had found their last resting place in Ireland in 1588—the year of the Armada.

Some distance from the shore there still lies a clutter of angle-irons, a pattern of nails and the guns of the three great ships—the full culverins, the demi-culverins, the sakers and the minions—all rusted and covered deep in sand and seaweed. There can be but little left of the timbers of these ships. The borings of millions of sea-worms through many centuries would have turned their timbers to brown powder that would have been washed up in millions of grains on Streeda strand.

One memento of this great sea-drama was retrieved. It was an elaborate figure-head of one of the ships, magnificently carved from the hardest of wood. Many years ago it came into the possession of a man named Simon Cullen, a prosperous businessman and Justice of the Peace in Sligo town. He built for himself a big house on the outskirts of the town. On the lawn which fronted it he placed the figure-head. Simon Cullen is dead for many years, and the figure-head is gone. Did the timber rot, or was it chopped up for firewood by the hand of a man who did not know that his axe was biting into the timber of history? We do not know, but today no one knows what became of the figure-head that was once mounted on the prow of a proud Armada vessel.

NOTE: In this chapter the word 'savages' has been used as a translation of the Spanish word *'salvajes'* which Captain Cuellar employed in his account. There have been a number of translations into English of Cuellar's letter. Some of the translators have softened the Spanish word for 'savages' into 'natives'. It is difficult to establish what Captain Cuellar meant by this description because word-meanings may have changed since the sixteenth century. Irish sensibilities may be pricked, but there can be little doubt that Captain Cuellar, accustomed as he was to a well-ordered society in which there was wealth, luxury and a high degree of education, must have found many of those Irish whom he met to be rough, uncouth and scarcely civilised.

CHAPTER ELEVEN

THE GHOUL WITH AN AXE

WILLIAM BURKE, of Ardnaree, near Ballina in the county of Mayo, must have been pleased in rendering service to her Majesty Queen Elizabeth. It must have been a swift journey over the track, which served as a highway through what was then known as 'Tyrawley', to a place between Killala and Belderg. That was the location of another wreck of a ship of the Spanish Armada. The exact place is not known, nor, strangely enough, is it remembered in tradition. William Burke was in time to capture 72 castaways from the ship.

In the State Papers of the Elizabethan era there are many statements which can be read only with a chill feeling of horror. In their cold recital of facts they sometimes cause revulsion. Such a document is that which Edward Whyte, Clerk of the Council of Connacht, wrote to his brother, Stephen, an alderman in Limerick. 'There is another great ship cast away in Tyrawley,' he began, 'and 72 of her men are taken by William Burke, of Ardnaree, and a bishop and a friar, and of the said number there be three noblemen. Most of the men of that ship are either slain or drowned. They were so miserably distressed coming to land that one man named Melaghlen McCabb killed eighty of them with his gallowglass axe.'

The fate of thousands of Spaniards who were wrecked on the Irish coast was tragic. But in no case was the fate as tragic or as terrible as that which met the Spaniards who came ashore at a spot between Killala and Belderg on that September day in 1588. It would have been a frightful scene as Melaghlen McCabb, the Scot and the ghoul with a gallowglass axe, waded knee-deep in the surf to redden the water with the blood of men who were crawling weakened and exhausted on to that Irish shore.

Eighty men died with appalling wounds before the maniacal
blood-lust of this savage was satiated, eighty men who
thought that in Ireland they would receive friendship, food
and shelter.

Those Spaniards who were noblemen, and who escaped
the murderous axe of Melaghlen McCabb, were sent to
Galway and were among those who were executed in that
city on the direct order of the Lord Deputy. On hearing
the news of the Mayo shipwreck, Sir Richard Bingham
once more sprang into rapacious action. 'He dispatched,'
stated a document, 'his cousins, George Bingham, the
younger, Francis Bingham, Robert Coker and Captain
Greene O'Molloy with commission to them and to Mr.
Comerford and Mr. Browne, of the Neale, for search to
be made in the baronies of the Owles and Erris to see
how the great ordnance and munitions might be saved.'
If their mission was successful there is no record of it,
and neither is there any record of a second shipwreck
on the north-west coast of Mayo which is strongly remembered in tradition. This ship, according to a story handed
down from generation to generation in Mayo families,
sank near Kid Island, a place of precipitous cliffs where
even a large vessel could founder without a single witness
to her wreck.

William Burke, of Ardnaree, may have been a faithful
servant of the Queen, but there was another Burke in Mayo
who was less loyal and Sir Richard Bingham kept a watchful
eye upon him lest he should shelter some forlorn band of
shipwrecked Spaniards. This scion of the Burkes merited
a special dispatch from Sir Richard to the Privy Council
in London. He wrote: 'The Devil's Hook (i.e. Richard Mc-
Rickard Burke) a notable malefactor of the Burkes of Mayo,
hath, of late, taken a dozen skiffs or small boats with certain
kearnes into the islands, by which should seem that they
have knowledge of some foreign enemy to land thereabouts,
for till now I have not heard of him a good while.'

The man who was called the Devil's Hook must have

been quite a formidable character for Sir Richard ended
his letter with the entreaty: 'Send me powder, lead and
match.' Despite the slaughter of the shipwrecked crews,
Sir Richard was displaying a most unsoldierly state of
anxiety—an anxiety which would not be allayed until
many more weeks had passed.

As this story moves to the coast of County Clare, it may
at this point pause to reflect on how speedily news was
brought to the Governor of Connacht and the Lord
Deputy. It could have been done only by relays of horsemen who rode through the day and night over the most
difficult country. Both these men appear to have been
perfectly informed about the number of shipwrecks, the
tonnage of the ships and the number of guns which they
carried. They were also well-informed on the exact locations
of the wrecks. All over the country there was a news-
collecting network. The number of reports which they
received showed Elizabethan bureaucracy at work. The
detail which these reports contained is an indication of
the efficiency of the English system of administration.
Even more remarkable is the survival in the State Papers
of so much documentation of the Armada story. These
letters and reports were carried about in pockets and in
pouches, opened and folded many times, read and re-read
until their edges were frayed and torn. They were put in
files, moved from place to place and often kept in damp
conditions. Yet after all these centuries they have survived
so that the story of what happened in Ireland in 1588
can be pieced together.

There is a document which tells that from the Clare coast
a large number of the Armada ships were sighted. Four
ships were seen to have anchored off Loop Head, and
probably two of these vessels were those which were wrecked
on this rock-bound coast. One of these was a ship of San
Sebastian. She was, in all probability, the *San Esteban,*
of 700 tons and carrying within her wooden hull 264 souls.
She came ashore at Doonbeg. Another large ship, which

may have been the 790-ton galleon *San Marcos* was
wrecked at Spanish Point where tradition places the wreck
on a reef inside Mutton Island. From this ship only four
survivors reached the shore. They fell into the hands of
George Cusack who held them captive until they were
claimed by the Sheriff of Clare who had the mellifluous
name of Boetius Clancy. The Sheriff was a brutal man.
All of these survivors were done to death. Sixty men
struggled ashore from the *San Esteban,* leaving behind them
a sea in which floated the corpses of 200 men.

All that week bodies and wreckage were being washed
ashore on the shoreline of Clare—not all of them from the
San Esteban or from the galleon which was probably
the *San Marcos.* In the Spanish records the words appear
opposite the names of many ships 'Lost in Ireland'. At
least twenty small vessels of the Armada are believed to
have perished far out in the Atlantic. These would have
been vessels used for despatch service or for inshore work.
They were unfitted for deep-sea sailing, these *zabras,*
fregatas and *pataches.* In the storms which followed in
quick succession these little vessels did not stand a chance
of survival. The wreckage and the bodies which were
washed ashore, according to tradition, at Ballaghaline,
near Doolin, County Clare, were perhaps silent evidence
of the fate of several of these little boats. The *San Marcos,*
however, was a big ship of the Squadron of Portugal.
She carried 33 heavy guns and 409 men sailed in her. She
and her crew had played a gallant part in the engagements
in the English Channel, especially at Gravelines where
she had fought beside the flag-ship of the Armada, the
San Martin. In this battle she had been so severely damaged
that her captain had been forced to pass cables under her
keel so that she was tied like a bundle in an effort to keep
her afloat. A ship in that condition was no match for the
heavy seas all the Armada vessels experienced in their run
down the north-west coast of Ireland.

Lingering in tradition is the story that Boetius Clancy

was cursed every seventh year for a century from the steps
of the altar in a church in Spain. The seven-year cursing
was a result of his cruelty towards the Spaniards who came
into his custody. Many of the survivors were brought
to his castle and there he hanged them. The place is called
Cnoc na Crochaire (Gallows Hill), and the spot where the
Spaniards were buried has since been named Tuama na
Spainneach. Many years afterwards, a local story tells,
there came to this place an old man and an old lady. They
were—the story goes—Spanish, and they sought to recover
the remains of their son. But they failed in their sad quest
because all those Spaniards so cruelly hanged had been
buried in a common pit-grave.

The crew of one Spanish ship which found shelter on
the coast of County Clare escaped the tender mercies of
Sheriff Boetius Clancy. He reported the arrival of this
vessel to Sir Richard Bingham in these words: 'One ship
is anchored in an unusual harbour called Liscannor, about
a mile westwards from Sir Turlough O'Brien's house. The
said ship has two cock-boats of which one broke from the
ship and landed. It is not like our cock-boats. It would
carry twenty men and it is painted red.'

It would seem that this boat had drifted ashore. Within
it Boetius found a large oil-jar and a piece of wood with
a brand mark which was clearly the Spanish royal mono-
gram—the Government brand. Boetius sent the oil-jar
and piece of wood to Sir Richard with the comment:
'There is some mystery hidden under this burn of three
letters.' He evidently thought that the brand was a cipher
which Sir Richard would be able to decode.

The ship was the galleass *Zuniga* which had set out from
Corunna many weeks before with 178 soldiers and 112
sailors and oarsmen on board. The men who sailed in
this vessel were indeed unfortunate. Eighty of them were
to die from thirst, hunger or food-poisoning. Their mis-
fortunes began at the point when the Duke of Medina
Sidonia decided that the Armada would sail home to Spain

in a wide arc which would avoid the dangers of the Irish coast. The *Zuniga* was not a vessel built for the Atlantic.

There were four galleasses included in the sailing strength of the Armada. In design they were long and narrow, and could be propelled by oars in addition to a spread of canvas. But against the ships of Queen Elizabeth's navy they were virtually useless. A single galleon of the Queen's fleet had more fire-power than all the galleasses which sailed with the Armada under the command of Hugo de Moncada. The galleasses sailed with an additional handicap. The guns were placed high above the water-line so that the oarsmen would not be impeded, but this design gave a high centre of gravity. A galleass could quickly capsize in a heavy sea.

The captain of the *Zuniga* must have been a resolute man. He must also have been one of the most skilful seamen of all those who sailed with the great Spanish fleet. At Gravelines, his was the vessel ordered to signal soundings. This meant that the *Zuniga* had to station herself closest to the shore. Against the powerful currents, the oarsmen, who were stripped to the waist, pulled at their heavy sweeps. They were close enough to see that the water was brown with the sand washed back from the beach as they strained to keep position and to carry out the orders of the Duke of Medina Sidonia. When the wind changed and the Armada was enabled to sail northwards, a feeling of relief was shared by those who sailed in the galleass. But worse dangers were to come.

On August 15 the *Zuniga* was in company with the rest of the fleet about seventy miles north-west of Rockall. Her captain would have felt little anxiety about his ability to keep station with the bigger ships. Then a heavy south-westerly wind drove all of them off-course. A succession of sloping green seas swept across the galleass and, as she shook herself free from the ponderous weight, her rudder splintered. At once signals of distress were sent fluttering for those on the flagship to see. No aid came from the

Duke. Neither did he order any of the other masters in the fleet to draw alongside the *Zuniga*.

Falling to the south-east, the galleass came upon the vessels which had stationed themselves upon Juan Martinez de Recalde's galleon, the *San Juan de Portugal*. To the mute appeal of the distress signals there came no response. It was a case of everyone looking after himself. The wind rose again, driving the crippled galleass before it until her log recorded that she was in latitude 63 north, many leagues west of the Faroes and not far distant was Iceland. By this time the men who were crowded within the wooden walls of the *Zuniga* had been without water for more than a week. Their provisions were either exhausted or uneatable. Many of them were showing signs of grave emaciation. Daily the bodies of those who succumbed to the dreadful conditions were pushed over the side to join in death those Spaniards for whom fathers and mothers, brothers and sisters, would grieve, but never know their last resting place.

Somewhere in those northern waters the crew repaired the rudder and with a more favourable wind the *Zuniga* rounded the tip of Ireland and began her run southwards. She survived the gale which caused so many other vessels to perish. After two days of grim battling to keep afloat, the crew found themselves off the Blaskets, but when the wind shifted suddenly to south, they found, after many hours sailing, that they were hemmed in by land. The *Zuniga* ran in towards Liscannor and found a safe anchorage there.

For these weakened men this part of the Irish coast must have presented a scene of wild and terrifying magnificence. For five miles tower the vertical bastions of the Cliffs of Moher, rising at their highest point to 668 feet above the sea. They are too steep to support plant life and they provide few ledges on which seabirds can rest or nest. They are grim and savage when the storm-winds beat upon them. At the base of these cliffs the Atlantic is rarely at rest, beating incessantly a rhythm of power, surf, and spume. For those who would approach from the north it would be a relief to round Hag's Head into Liscannor Bay, at the head of which there is a sandy estuary.

As the *Zuniga* lay in this 'unusual harbour' the cold eyes of Boetius Clancy kept a watchful vigil. His chance came when the second of the small boats left the Spanish vessel and headed for the shore. Clancy and his men swooped upon the boat as it grounded, but captured only the purser of the galleass, Pietro Baptista of Naples. His companions rowed swiftly back to the ship—now convinced that in that part of Ireland they could not expect to find safety. The calm water of the anchorage enabled them to repair sails, rigging and rudder. The oars made it possible for the ship to move down the bay into the open sea once more where they picked up a strong north-easterly wind—the same wind which helped other Spanish ships to sail away from a coast on which so many of their fellow-countrymen had died.

If the crew of the *Zuniga* were jubilant at their escape, they could not have foreseen the other miseries to which they would be subjected. The vessel was taking water as she passed the mouth of the English Channel with a westerly wind filling her torn sails. The captain steered for Le Havre.

The *Zuniga* arrived at the French port none too soon, crewed by men who were virtually living skeletons—men who could not stand without the support of rope or capstan and who craved food and water. When they had recovered sufficient strength they set about making everything ship-shape again. Material for repairs was obtained from Calais where a sister-galleass had grounded. And from Calais, too, came provisions and 56 men. In addition, twenty men of three nationalities who had escaped from Ireland were taken on board—men who had been stripped of everything they possessed.

After what seemed endless delays, many of which were caused by the interchange of diplomatic letters between the French and Spanish courts, the *Zuniga* was allowed to sail in the middle of April in the year 1589. One could be forgiven for thinking that the *Zuniga* was an unlucky vessel. She had been but a few hours at sea when a fierce wind swept the Channel to toss the ship hither and thither, rending her newly-patched sails and battering her weakened hull. After many hours in which those on board thought that their last hour had come, the *Zuniga* was blown back to the port she had left. More weeks were passed in repairing the damage caused by the storm. Then, driven to the limits of their patience and endurance, the crew mutinied and finally streamed ashore to desert.

For two months the *Zuniga* lay at Le Havre until she began to silt up at her berth. She did return to Spain, and eventually to her home port of Naples—so long overdue that she had been listed as one of the ships of the Armada which 'perished in Ireland'.

At the time when the *Zuniga* was nosing her way into Liscannor Bay, seven ships of the Armada—four galleons and three *zabras*, or despatch boats, entered the mouth of the Shannon and sailed up-river to an anchorage at Scattery Roads. This was, indeed, good pilotage. The group of ships was too powerful to attack. The English could only watch and await developments. From one of the galleons a boat was sent to Kilrush to whose inhabitants a cask of wine was offered for casks of fresh water. For several days the Spaniards swung at this safe anchorage while the repair work on their vessels continued under the eyes of Queen Elizabeth's officers.

These Spaniards must have been severely weakened by untended wounds, hunger, thirst and fever. They had on board hundreds of well-armed soldiers, men who could have swept aside any force which the English planters might have brought against them in that part of the country. But these superbly trained men were so weakened that they were never used to take what they required in food and water by force of arms. There is evidence of a landing from the ships, but it appears to have been so feeble that it was easily checked. To such a state of weakness had the proud soldiers of Spain been reduced that they offered to the Queen's officer, Nicholas Cahane, an entire ship, the *Annunciada,* with all her gear and guns in return for fresh provisions and material to make repairs. He refused. In the offer of the Spaniards there was an apparent admission of desperation.

A few days later Nicholas Cahane must have congratulated himself on having refused the offer. The ship which was to have figured in the exchange was stripped of everything that could be transferred at the anchorage and then set on fire. She was so badly damaged and leaking to such an extent that she could not stay afloat much longer. The captain of this vessel was Ohmucevic Iveglia, a famous Ragusan seaman who had the status of Admiral and about whom many details have been discovered in recent research in the Maritime Museum of Dubrovnik. (Hundreds of Dalmatians took part in the attempt to invade England). The entire company of the ship, which burned to the waterline before the blackened hulk sank to the bottom of the Shannon estuary, were taken on board the *Barca de Danzig*. All the ships sailed together from the Shannon on a brisk north-east wind on September 11.

The safe return to Spain of the *Barca de Danzig* was recorded in Spain, and it is highly probable that the other vessels in whose company she sailed likewise made a landfall on the Spanish coast. They were fortunate that among their pilots was a man who evidently had an exact knowledge of the Irish coastline and its safer anchorages.

CHAPTER TWELVE

THE NOBLE COMPANY

FOR ALMOST two weeks *La Rata Santa Maria Encoronada* had been pitching and rolling in about 58 degrees north, while the wind howled in a succession of storms. The wind came from the south-west, the worst possible quarter for those who sailed in this great ship of the Armada. Somewhere in the surging waste of slate-grey water were the other ships of the mighty fleet—but where? *La Rata Santa Maria Encoronada* lurched on with 419 souls on board. She was one of the ships that had lost contact with the flagship of the Armada—now she could no longer stay afloat. As the gales continued it became obvious to even the soldiers who sailed in her that shelter would have to be sought to caulk seams and to repair rigging and sails. *La Rata* ran for the Irish coast.

Unseen by the look-outs at bow and stern, four other ships of the Squadron of the Levant, and four more powerful ships of the Armada, an Andalusian, a Castilian, and two from the Guipuzcoan squadron had taken the same course at the same time. *La Rata* had not been built for war. She was a big Mediterranean merchant ship of the type called a carrack, a design which had high bow and stern castles and capacious holds. To take her place in the invasion-fleet she had been fitted with 35 guns.

She was, for a number of reasons, an unusual vessel. Among those 419 soldiers, sailors, gunners and servants who peered through the sea-mist at the dark shadow on the horizon which was the coast of Ireland, there was a gay, debonair and brave young man named Don Alonso Martinez de Leyva, a man of noble birth and one-time Captain-General of the Cavalry of Milan. In the list which the Duke of Medina Sidonia prepared of those who sailed with the Armada, Don Alonso Martinez de Leyva is recorded as a mere gentleman volunteer. But he was more than that. He was a dashing and experienced soldier, a young man with an engaging and magnetic personality, handsome and strong—and a favourite of King Philip, who, it is thought, had given secret orders that the youthful Don would succeed the commander-in-chief of the Armada should the Duke of Medina Sidonia be killed.

It was to be expected that among the noble families of
Spain there should be keen competition to be numbered
among those who sailed with Don Alonso. There would
be reputations for gallantry to be won, there would be
for second and third sons an opportunity of acquiring
new estates and new wealth and possessions. All this
would be done under the leadership of a courageous young
leader who stood in high favour with their King. Thus
it came about that in the *La Rata Santa Maria Encoronada*
there sailed the flower of Spanish chivalry, scores of
adventurous young men who were scions of the noblest
and the most ancient families of Spain.

The carrack *La Rata* was a vessel of the Squadron of
the Levant, which was under the command of Martin de
Bertendona. Yet it does appear that Don Alonso de
Leyva was accepted by the Duke of Medina Sidonia as
an equal to the other squadron commanders and a leader
who had a right to be present at the decision-making
councils which the Duke held so frequently. In the fighting
between Eddystone and Start Point, *La Rata* was always
in the station of greatest importance and greatest danger.
In the council which met on board the flagship in northern
waters, it was de Leyva who put the view that the fleet
should sail to Norway for repairs and re-grouping before
starting on the homeward run to Spain. Spanish records
of the Channel engagements imply that the young nobleman
was the real commander of the Squadron of the Levant.
A tragic fate was to overcome this gallant and noble
company. All of them were to die. And among them was
a young Irishman who was also of noble birth—Maurice,
son of James Fitzmaurice who had been elected leader
by the Munster Geraldines in their struggle against the
expropriations of the English, and who had been forced
to leave for Spain in 1575.

During the time that the remnant of the Armada was
beating down the Irish coast, the wind that blew
most strongly and frequently came from the south.

If it varied, it veered from south to south-west.

Despite this ill-wind, many of the vessels made their way to windward and with difficulty maintained a southerly course—proving that they were able to sail within six points of the wind. Other ships were not so well-suited for these storm-tossed waters and they only made way when they got wind abaft the beam. One of these was *La Rata Santa Maria Encoronada* which in every gale had to run with scant sail. She was one of those ships which had not the inbuilt qualities of design to escape the great wedge of land—the north-westerly promontory of County Mayo. Yet she was so skilfully handled that she weathered Erris Head and Benwee Head. And there she was trapped. Confronting them was the Mullet Peninsula, that narrow isthmus which separates Broadhaven, on the north, from the deeper and larger Bay of Blacksod. The Bay of Blacksod is ringed by low and rather desolate shores on either side, but Broadhaven is carved into a bolder coastline. The Spaniards saw this remote peninsula of the Mullet with its sand and its bogs, its treeless, windswept and lonely landscape, and they saw it hammered by a turbulent and raging sea. In summer this is a place of pleasant charm as the light shimmers in the reflection of the vast ocean. But when storms rage it can be the very distillation of desolation. Today two lighthouses on this stretch of coast warn the sailor of the dangers of the Mullet—one on Eagle Island on the north, and one on Black Rock on the south. Between them lie twin islands— mere reefs upon which the waves pound in stormy weather. The Spaniards had no lighthouses to guide them in 1588, no charts to lay bare the perils of this indented coast. Around them there was a heaving sea and the veils of rain-clouds closed their circle of visibility. All they had was a fervent hope that God would take them safely away from this fearful shoreline.

On the night of September 6-7, 1588, *La Rata Santa Maria Encoronada* anchored in Blacksod Bay between

Tiraun and Ballycroy. The trouble which beset other ships of the Armada also plagued the commander of this great ship, for she had few anchors, and what cable she had was frayed and weak. When the wind got up once more she began to drag her anchors and finally she jolted with a crash on to the shelving strand of Ballycroy.

All her crew got safely ashore. At once, under the leadership of Don Alonso de Leyva, they took over the castles of Ballycroy and Doolough, fortifying them as they well knew how to do. From their stranded ship they removed all the guns, armour, stores and treasure. When that was done they set *La Rata Santa Maria Encoronada* on fire. Up to quite modern times, when tides were exceptionally low, pieces of sand-buried timbers from this ship could be recovered, all burned at one end in proof of the manner in which she had been destroyed.

Don Alonso and his men did not stay long at Ballycroy. He led them to the Mullet, and there they established themselves in Tiraun castle near Elly Bay. After a day or two the Spaniards were surprised to see a large group of their fellow-countrymen wending their way towards them. These were the men who had been on board a ship which had been wrecked at Inver, in Broadhaven. This vessel found itself immortality in the epic folklore tales of the district as *an long maol* (the bare ship), because it came into the broad bay mastless and, therefore, without sail of any kind. Should anyone believe in stories of vast hoards of Spanish gold on the north-west coast of Ireland, there is material in the accounts which have been handed down from father to son about this nameless ship. The seanachies tell of a great treasure from this vessel which was entrusted to an Irish simpleton by the crew when they came ashore. The instructions he received were to bury the treasure in a safe and secret place. He did so 'in a bog between two strands just under the moon'. So far no one has discovered even a single golden coin of this treasure— a fact which is not surprising.

Yet one should not dismiss folklore too lightly. There may not have been rich treasure on *an long maol,* but on board *La Rata* were noblemen who would have followed the custom of their time in bringing gold and silver plate, richly jewelled ornaments, and, certainly a greater amount of gold and silver coins than would have been found on any other ship in the Armada. They went to war in great state in those days—Don Alonso, in fact, was accompanied by no fewer than 36 servants. The other young noblemen would also have had many servitors, depending on their rank.

When Don Alonso de Leyva had been some days at Tiraun, two other ships of the Armada sailed into Blacksod Bay and anchored. One of them was the *Nuestra Senora de Begona,* a merchant vessel of 750 tons and with 297 men on board. The other was a transport, *Duquesa Santa Ana,* a ship of 900 tons, armed with 23 guns, and carrying 357 men. All who had escaped from the wrecks of *La Rata Santa Maria Encoronada* and the ship which figures in folklore as *an long maol* were taken on board the *Duquesa Santa Ana.* On a day when the wind was favourable this over-loaded vessel sailed out of the bay and headed northwards in the hope of making a landfall in Scotland. She was destined for shipwreck, but the master of the *Nuestra Senora de Begona* made a wiser choice, perhaps because his ship was less damaged. He sailed some days later for Spain and the vessel is listed among those which returned to Santander.

Sir Richard Bingham showed the utmost reluctance in sending a force against the Spaniards who had spent many days at Blacksod and Broadhaven. The news that six hundred well-armed Spaniards had landed and had fortified castles on the coast may have deterred him in taking more vigorous action. He was well-informed about the landings, but his only action appears to have been to ask the Lord Deputy to send him reinforcements, a request he had made earlier without result.

Edward Whyte's report to the Privy Council in London makes it clear that Sir Richard was perfectly aware of the landings, the number of ships and the number of men. He wrote: 'A ship was cast ashore at Ballycroy and 600 came ashore to fortify the castle. Don Alonso de Leyva was chief. Two days before the ship was lost, the master, Giovanni Avancini, and fourteen Italians went ashore in the cock-boat which they abandoned and marched inland, but Richard Burke, called the Devil's son, robbed them and made them prisoners. Don Alonso used empty casks to float some men ashore to fetch back the cock-boat.'

Giovanni Avancini may have decided that it was better to die on land than to be drowned at sea when he marched away from the coast and into captivity. He and his fourteen companions were among those executed in Athlone.

In the wavering script of Edward Whyte, preserved after many centuries, yet still as clear as the day the words were penned in 1588, is the sad story of the death of an Irish exile who planned to fight for his native country in the army of another nation. The exile was young Maurice Fitzmaurice, and Edward Whyte recorded it thus: 'Sir Richard Bingham was given to understand by one of the prisoners brought from Erris that Maurice Fitzmaurice, son to the late arch-traitor, James Fitzmaurice, was dead in the great ship which lay before Tiraun and was cast into the sea in a fair cypress chest with great solemnity.' And so that is how this young exile died and was buried—within sight of the land of his Norman-Irish forbears. It was a tragic end to a tragic period in Irish history. Edward Whyte, ever-watchful chronicler of events that occurred in his jurisdiction as Clerk of the Council of Connacht, wrote the final words on the events at Ballycroy. He reported tersely: 'Mr. Gerald Comerford, her Majesty's attorney in Connacht, informed Sir Richard Bingham that the ship that was at Pollilly by Tiraun has sailed—taking the company that was wrecked. James Blake and Thomas Burke McNabb took out of the wreck a boatful of treasure, cloth of gold and velvet.' The vultures, evidently, had descended when those they feared had departed.

As the possessions which had been left behind were being displayed on the lonely shore at Tiraun, Don Alonso de Leyva and his companions on board the *Duquesa Santa Ana* began once more to experience the ill-luck which had attended the enterprise of the great Armada. A storm swept down upon them. Conditions on board must have been extraordinarily crowded, for she now carried 800 men. Buffeted by the wind which screamed through the taut rigging, the *Duquesa Santa Ana* passed the entrance to Donegal Bay in safety, but shortly afterwards she was blown inshore and wrecked in Loughros Bay.

Don Alonso de Leyva might have been forgiven if he had let his head sink into his hands in utter despair. Twice had this awful and treacherous coast claimed the ships on which he sailed. But mercifully the events of the future were hidden from him. Before the month had ended he would be shipwrecked a third time—and on the third time he would die.

When the *Duquesa Santa Ana* grounded at a place which tradition identifies, all of those who sailed in her got safely ashore. They were fully armed, well-rested and fed with provisions which they had obtained at Tiraun in Mayo. They would be more than a match for any English force which might be sent against them. Their fear of being attacked was groundless, for the dauntless North was virtually unconquered and they were among friends.

It will be conceded that Don Alonso was a man upon whom fortune did not smile. He received a leg injury before the ship was driven ashore, and, strangely enough, this information is given by an Irishman who was on board the *Duquesa Santa Ana*. His name was James Machary (or McGarry) 'from the Cross, in the County of Tipperary'. He was a seaman who fell into the hands of the English after he had decided that he had had enough of seafaring

on board Spanish ships. In an examination by Lord
Deputy Fitzwilliam he described how he had been impressed
into the Armada while he was at Lisbon. He sailed as
a member of the crew of the *Duquesa Santa Ana,* a ship
which he called Flemish. He described how his ship
had picked up the survivors of the two shipwrecks in
County Mayo, 'taking with them all the goods they had—
plate, apparel, money, jewels and weapons'. He told the
Lord Deputy how Don Alonso had been injured by a
capstan 'so that he could neither go nor ride', and he added
'Don Alonso was tall, slender, of fair complexion with
flaxen smooth hair, mild-tempered and greatly revered by
the whole company.' Having played his part in the Armada
—a part which may not have been so unwillingly under-
taken as he gave the Lord Deputy to believe, James
Machary passed into history as another of those Irishmen
who were always to be found where there was fighting
to be done.

For nine days Don Alonso and his company stayed on
the shore of Loughros Bay. The fair-haired leader was
in great pain, but he continued to direct preparations to
withstand attack until word was brought to him that in
Killybegs harbour, in Donegal Bay to the south, a Spanish
ship had anchored. With great speed they broke camp and
set off on a march to Killybegs, Don Alonso being carried
in an improvised litter.

Three ships had been forced into Killybegs. One almost
made a safe anchorage, but her leaking seams had so
filled her holds with water that she sank at the harbour
mouth. A second ship crushed her timbers on rocks,
drifted for a while, once more crashed on to a submerged
reef and she was pounded to pieces by the powerful surge
of the Atlantic. The third vessel was a gallant little ship—
the galleass *Gerona.* This was the vessel of which Don
Alonso had received news. She had been battered and
mauled by a succession of gales, but she could still float
and she could sail. Her galleass design also gave the

advantage that, if needed, she could be propelled by oars.

The men in the *Gerona* and the men who had marched from Loughros Bay received all the assistance which MacSweeney Bannagh—one of the most courageous of the Irish chieftains—could give them. Men of Donegal laboured with the men of Spain to fit the *Gerona* for sea. In the storm which had overtaken her before she entered Killybegs harbour, the hammering of the waves had smashed her rudder. Timber from one of the vessels that had run aground was used in the work of repair, and within two weeks the *Gerona* was deemed fit to return to sea. It was mid-October when the little vessel moved out to meet once more the Atlantic swell.

If MacSweeney Bannagh had been generous and hospitable to the unfortunate Spaniards, Sir John O'Doherty did not follow his example. Sir John, a powerful chieftain in this rugged section of the country, had at this time much of his power curtailed and had evidently decided to provide no aid for the Spaniards. O'Doherty complained to Lord Deputy Fitzwilliam that 'MacSweeney, having kept 3,000 Spaniards until his own country was consumed, directed the Spaniards for hate into my country to consume it too.' The Lord Deputy had other channels of information about the Armada survivors at Killybegs. Mr. Henry Duke quickly reported: 'There were 2,400 Spaniards in the country of the MacSweeneys. They have left with MacSweeney an Irish friar called James Ne Dowrough who went into Spain with James Fitzmaurice.' The friar never fell into the hands of the Lord Deputy and it is reasonable to suppose that he was hidden and sheltered by the redoubtable and courageous MacSweeneys. They, however, had their traducers, for William Taafe reported that the MacSweeneys had killed forty Spaniards 'as soon as the rest had gone aboard ship'. This report was manifestly untrue.

Slowly and with much pitching and rolling in waves that seemed to be steep cliffs of Connemara marble, so

heavy was their impact on her frail hull, the *Gerona* sailed
past Lough Swilly and Lough Foyle. Soon she would
round the northmost tip of Ireland and set her prow
towards Scotland. But this was not to be. On a night
which brought with the sunset a fierce gale, the *Gerona*
gave up her long struggle against the Atlantic. Great
waves broke against her rudder and as the timber splintered,
the deck took a steep angle. From that moment the vessel
and the 1,300 men who crowded her superstructure, and
who were crammed into every foot of space below-deck,
were doomed. With a feeling of the appalling inevitability
of approaching death they heard over the screaming of
the wind the deep growl of waves on a rocky coast. A
mighty crash was followed by a rending and tearing of timber.
The *Gerona* had been driven ashore at Dunluce, County
Antrim, at a point known ever since as Port na Spainneach.

Within an hour all of that noble company had perished
with the exception of nine men who were washed ashore
more dead than alive. They were brought to the chieftain
Sorley Boy McDonnell who cared for them well in the
great castle of which the ruins still remain on the clifftop
at Dunluce. There he tended those who had been injured,
and when they had recovered from their ordeal he arranged
for them to sail to Scotland.

Lord Deputy Fitzwilliam reported to Queen Elizabeth
after this tragic shipwreck in which died the flower of
Spanish chivalry, the wealthy and the brave: 'Three fair
pieces of brass (i.e. cannon) doth lie among the rocks
at Bunboyes where Don Alonso was drowned and can be
recovered.' He had written too optimistically, because
Sorley Boy McDonnell had been there before him and
had dragged the guns to Dunluce castle where they were
mounted on the battlements. Two chests of treasure were
also salvaged, but about these the Lord Deputy was
prudently silent. Queen Elizabeth would have dealt out
summary punishment to those who had allowed Spanish
treasure to fall into the hands of the mere Irish.

Two hundred and sixty bodies were washed ashore.
They were buried with the great petrified lava-mass of the
Giant's Causeway as their memorial so long as the world
shall last. The remainder sank beneath the water to find
a last resting place that can never be marked.

CHAPTER THIRTEEN

THE BROKEN PLEDGE

LORD BURGHLEY broke the seal on a letter that had come
from Ireland. The message it contained gave him grim
pleasure, for Sir William Fitzwilliam, by the end of
September, 1588, had shed many of his fears and jubilantly
reported to his masters in London: 'God hath fought by
shipwreck, savages and famine for her Majesty against
these proud Spaniards.' The Lord Deputy of Ireland
might have added that the proud Spaniards had also been
massacred despite a solemn promise that they would be
conducted unharmed into his presence in Dublin. But of
this he made no mention in his letter to Lord Burghley.

The Spaniards who were to die after a pledge had been
shamefully and treacherously broken were on board *La
Trinidad Valencera*, a great ship of 1,000 tons, and one
of those luckless vessels which sailed in the Squadron of
the Levant. She was heavily armed with 42 guns and she
had sailed from Corunna with 360 men. With shattered
spars and torn canvas, and with a weight of water in her
store-rooms and hold which the pumps could not control,
La Trinidad Valencera closed the coast of Donegal. As
the water within the hull rose inch by inch, her master
sailed through Inishtrahull Sound and along the shoreline
of Inishowen until he brought his vessel to anchor in
Glenagivney Bay. Everything that experienced seamen
could do was done to keep the great ship afloat, but her

list became steeper with every hour. There came a moment when it was imperative to give the order to abandon ship, for *La Trinidad Valencera* would never sail again.

The story of this vessel is unusual. Her owner was the Grand Duke of Tuscany who had caused her to be built and had armed her with guns that were the heaviest and most powerful in comparison with any other vessel that sailed the Mediterranean. He named her *Balanzara*. With that name on her prow below a richly carved figurehead, he sailed to Lisbon to load a valuable cargo of spice, pepper, cloves and cinnamon. Such a rich cargo would be safe in this large merchantman so heavily armed.

The *Balanzara* was never returned to her rightful owner. She was requisitioned by the Marquis of Santa Cruz to strengthen the fighting core of galleons in the Enterprise of England, and, re-named *La Trinidad Valencera,* she sailed with the Armada.

At a point off the Donegal coast the look-outs on this big vessel saw another ship of the Armada in dire distress. This was the *Barca de Amburgo*, a transport of 600 tons, armed with 23 guns and carrying 264 men. The *Barca de Amburgo* was so waterlogged that her survival in such heavy seas was a matter of amazement, mixed with gratitude to God, in the minds of those who sailed in her. All of them were transferred to the deck of *La Trinidad Valencera* before the transport foundered. They did not know it then, but they had been rescued from one danger to become enmeshed in another that would bring about their death.

Other ships with weakened and dying crews also ran for the coast of Donegal. One of them approached the cluster of islands which are collectively known as The Rosses. This vessel struck at a place known ever since as Carraig na Spainneach, at Mullaghderg, near Kincasslagh, on a rocky coast with many hidden shoals and sunken reefs. She sank in comparatively shallow water—so shallow that in 1797 a group of young men engaged in salvage operations. They raised a quantity of lead and a number of brass guns, one of which was ten feet long. These were broken up and sold for scrap at 4½d. a lb. The iron guns, of which they found a number, were left in the water. A number of Spanish gold coins were also recovered by the young divers. In 1895 a search was made for this ship from a small steamer named *The Harbour Lights*, but nothing was found save the sand-covered hulk.

Two miles south of Carraig na Spainneach, in Arranmore Roads, and close to Rinn a' Chaislean, another Armada vessel was wrecked. In 1853, Mr. Richard Heard, chief officer of the coastguards in Tirconnaill, made a salvage attempt at the place where this ship foundered. They recovered an anchor which was sent to London where it was presented to the United Services Institution.

The anchor is one of the few reminders of the Armada recovered from the sunken ships on the Irish coast, but among them may be listed a bell in the parish church of Carndonagh, County Donegal, which tradition says was salvaged from a ship of the Spanish fleet wrecked at Inishowen. It bears the legend: *'Sancta Maria, Ora Pro Nobis—Richardus Pottar'*, with his sign or trade mark.

Salvage attempts in search of Spanish gold are nothing new. They began a few weeks after the shipwrecks on the Clare coast when Sir George Carew, Master of Ordnance, was plaintively telling the Privy Councillors that efforts to recover some cannon were proving costly, 'because the necessity of sustaining the divers with copious draughts of usequebagh'.

Survivors of these shipwrecks were brought to Sorley Boy McDonnell, or directed to the house of the Bishop of Derry, Redmond O'Gallagher, the same bishop who had given hospitality and shelter to Captain Cuellar.

Sorley Boy McDonnell was no friend of the English. In his hatred of the men who sought to rule his territory in Antrim in the name of Queen Elizabeth he had good reason. A few short years before—in 1575—the Earl

of Essex had attacked his territory. The chieftain
sent part of his family, and many of the women and
children of his followers, to Rathlin Island where, he
thought, they would be safe. The news of this was quickly
brought to Essex who directed Sir John Norris to lead a
strong force of soldiers which landed on the island. It
was a simple military exercise for these soldiers to attack
the castle on the island. The defenders capitulated after
a siege of a few hours—and more than 200 defenceless
people within its walls were put to the sword.

The hunt for 400 terrorised people—mostly women and
children—which followed is one of the most horrifying
episodes in Irish history—even when allowances are made
for the accepted brutalities of the sixteenth century and the
coarseness of mind which made them possible. These
weak and defenceless women and children were butchered,
while from the mainland Sorley Boy McDonnell watched
the carnage, helpless and half-demented by the frightfulness
of it all. The English historian, Froude, described those
who died as 'chiefly mothers and their little ones'. Queen
Elizabeth was graciously pleased to send to Sir John Norris
her compliments and thanks for 'this well-devised
enterprise'.

Sorley Boy, the indomitable chieftain of the North,
who was enabled to hold out so long against English efforts
to subjugate him by the huge forests which covered much
of his territory at the time, may also have given succour
to the survivors of a vessel which is briefly mentioned in
the State Papers. This vessel, according to a letter which
has been preserved, 'is at Donegal and it was saved by
means of a boat that was sent to them from the shore,
but they lost their mainmast and they cast out 120 great
horses and sixty mules.' Of this ship no other details have
been recorded in the State papers. Without a mainmast,
it is unlikely that she could have been repaired to enable
her to make a passage back to Spain.

The tragedy in which all those who sailed in *La Trinidad*

Valencera were enmeshed is comparatively well-documented so that a clear picture can be built up. When the vessel moved inshore and anchored in Glenagivney Bay she was sinking. The man in command was Don Alonso de Luzon, leader of an infantry brigade or *tercio*. Five *tercios* sailed in the Armada and they were composed of professional soldiers, reputed to be the best soldiers in Europe at that time. Each was commanded by a *maestro de campo* or colonel.

Don Alonso de Luzon has described how he first set foot on Irish soil. After his capture there was an examination by English interrogators. This account reads: 'They (Don Alonso and five others) landed with rapiers in their hands, whereupon they found four or five savage people who bade them welcome and used them well until some twenty more wild men came unto them, after which time they took away a bag of money containing 100 reals of plate and a blue cloak richly laid with gold lace.'

It was a luckless start, but worse was to follow. The small boat in which they had come ashore was leaking. For the payment of 200 ducats, plus a quantity of clothing, the Irish supplied them with a second small boat in which the men who crowded the decks of *La Trinidad Valencera* were ferried to the shore.

The transfer of 560 men from the great ship—200 had been taken from the *Barca de Amburgo*—occupied two days. The first to be landed were groups of the wounded and the sick, about a hundred in all. On the seventh trip between ship and shore the only small-boat which the Spaniards possessed sank and all its occupants were drowned. Among those who were ferried ashore were the master of *La Trinidad Valencera,* Don Beltran del Salto, and the master of the *Barca de Amburgo,* Jaques Flamenco. It was a well-armed band which set off on a march inland, although they were weak and emaciated. Food was difficult to obtain, as the report of Don Alonso de Luzon's examination stated: 'They found no other relief of victual in the country than for certain horses which they bought off poor men for their money, which horses they killed and did eat—and some small quantity of butter which the common people also brought to sell.'

The long column of Spanish castaways marched unmolested until they came to the fortified home of Sir John O'Doherty at Ellagh. There they encountered a strong force of soldiers led by Richard and Henry Hovenden, foster-brothers of Hugh O'Neill, Earl of Tyrone. Weary, dispirited and hungry after their march of seven days through the rough countryside, the Spaniards began a parley with the Hovenden brothers. The result was that the Spaniards agreed to surrender. Still preserved is the report of the interrogation of Don Alonso in which it is stated: 'Don Alonso de Luzon said they yielded themselves to the captains who carried the Queen's ensigns, O'Donnell and his wife being present, upon condition that their lives would be spared until they came to the Lord Deputy, and that they should be suffered to repair unto him, every private soldier with one suit of apparel and every gentleman with two. They laid down 350 muskets and calivers, and some few pikes to her Majesty's use. All were seized by John Kelly, whom they term Sergeant-Major, and who is Captain Richard Hovenden's lieutenant, after which the promise was not kept with them, but the soldiers and savage people spoiled them of all they had.'

The noblemen, the ships' captains and the military leaders, including Don Alonso, were then separated from the rank and file. It happened at a place which is marked today by the ruined castle at Ellagh, on the north side of the railway which once connected Derry and Buncrana. It is a place in which ghosts may walk, ghosts which may cry out in agony and in terror, for the grass around this castle was dewed with the blood of men who were savagely murdered by captors who had solemnly pledged to spare their lives. It is a black chapter in Irish history, unredeemed by any pretence of excuse.

On the night which followed the surrender, Richard and Henry Hovenden led an attack against these defenceless Spaniards and butchered them without mercy. In a scene of appalling frightfulness 300 men were massacred and a mere 150 escaped by running blindly through bog, furze and scrub. These half-naked wretches were found by the people of what is now the townland of Baloor, sheltered, fed and hidden until they could be secretly sent on their way to Bishop O'Gallagher or to Sorley Boy McDonnell. Others found a refuge with MacSweeney at Doe castle.

The treachery with which they had dealt with their captives is not revealed by the brutal Hovendens in their subsequent report to Lord Deputy Fitzwilliam. They told the Lord Deputy: 'We came up with the Spaniards in a village called Ellagh, and we sent an emissary to learn who they were and what were their intentions in thus invading a part of the dominions of her Majesty the Queen. They made answer that they had come with the intention of invading England and formed part of the Armada, and that they had been obliged to land by stress of weather in this place. Having heard this answer, and seeing that they were more than 600 men, we encamped at nightfall at a distance of a musket shot, we not being more than 140. Towards midnight we began skirmishing with them for about two hours, killing the *tiente de campo* and more than 200 men besides, causing them moreover, much loss in wounded without our having lost more than one man.'

The Hovendens appear to have been inspired by the same motive which actuated other servants of the Queen in Ireland, namely to impress upon those at the Head Office of the Great Joint Stock Company, which was the England of those days, that they were loyal and enthusiastic shareholders who hoped to benefit by a show of zeal in promoting the interests of the company. In describing their perfidious massacre of unarmed men as 'a skirmish at

midnight', they hoped, perhaps, to show themselves as
courageous soldiers who had defeated a *tercio* of Spaniards
although greatly outnumbered. It is unlikely that they feared
punishment for their barbarous action. The reputation
of Lord Deputy Fitzwilliam was not one of amiable kindness
towards the Irish, or towards anyone else who might
threaten to weaken the rule of the Queen in Ireland. The
report which the Lord Deputy sent to London makes no
mention of the mass-murder. He told the Privy Council:
'It is reported that a great number of Spaniards that were
stripped naked by the soldiers that serve under both the
Hovendens are now come to the other Spaniards that
landed in MacSweeney's country, and thither brought
by the Bishop of Derry—a most seditious Papist and a
man very like to procure great aid to the Spaniards if
he can.'

Those who escaped the bloodstained swords of the
Hovenden brothers were sent to Scotland. On their return
to Spain they told the Pilot-General of the Armada that
they had been wrecked close to the Blaskets. These were
sailors who had probably seen the Kerry coast on other
voyages, and, mistaking their landfall, had assumed
that the Garvan Islands and Inishtrahull were the Blaskets.
Their good fortune in returning to their homeland was not
shared by the 45 noblemen and officers who had been
separated from their men before the 'midnight skirmish'.
These men were forced to take part in a death-march to
Drogheda and their number was fewer at the end of that
long journey to the east coast. The part which O'Donnell,
Earl of Tyrconnell, played in the suffering of the Spaniards
is not one of which Irishmen can be proud.

Yet an explanation may be found for his supine attitude
towards the English forces which were, apparently, strong
in his territory. There is also the powerful factor that his
son, the legendary Red Hugh, was at that time held as
hostage in Dublin castle. These circumstances may offer
an explanation for O'Donnell's inactivity in protecting

the Spaniards who landed in his territory. But he did
more than to stand as a passive spectator—he accompanied
his Spanish prisoners on the trek across the country.
When he arrived at Dublin Castle he handed over the
small group that had survived, with a plea that his loyalty
to the Queen had been proved and that his son should be
released. As we now know, this plea was not granted
and Red Hugh did not gain his freedom until that night
of snow and frost when he made an escape that has
thrilled every schoolboy in Ireland whenever the story is
told.

The effort of the father to obtain the release of his
hostage-son is dismissed in the Elizabethan State Papers
in these words: 'O'Donnell is lately come up with a company of thirty Spaniards and is a suitor for the liberty of
his son, now pledged in the castle of Dublin.'

From O'Neill (at this time Turlough Lynagh O'Neill)
came a growl of anger which was reported by Geoffrey
Fenton, Clerk of the Council in Dublin. He wrote: 'O'Neill
hath bitterly reproved O'Donnell, saying that he and his
posterity may seek a dwelling in another country for
having betrayed the Spaniards their only refuge.' O'Neill,
in fact, did everything in his power to aid the Spaniards
and sent a herd of cattle for their use into Tyrconnell.
So defiant was O'Neill in providing a refuge for the castaways that the Lord Deputy reported to London: 'The
Spaniards are so favoured and succoured by the country
people as it will be hard to hunt them out, and with long
time and great labour.'

The 45 captive survivors from *La Trinidad Valencera*
suffered great hardship in their march to Dublin. Fifteen
of them died on the way. This toll of death may have
prompted the Hovenden brothers to write to the Lord
Deputy with a request for transport, telling him that the
prisoners were weak and unable to march.

At Drogheda the prisoners were met by an interrogator
sent by the Lord Deputy, and, as usual, the probing for

loot formed a major part in the questioning. Don Alonso
de Luzon did not know what money, jewels, plate and
apparel had been taken from the whole company, 'but
for his own part, he lost in plate, jewellery, money and
apparel that was taken from his servants about the value
of 3,000 ducats, but who took the same he knoweth not.'
He had been told by one of his men that 'he who termed
himself Sergeant-Major to the two Captains took his
plate which was worth 1,000 ducats or more.'

Don Alonso told his inquisitor that because they were
too weak from illness, four of the ship's company had
stayed behind in O'Donnell's country—Don Alvaro de
Mendoza, Don Antonio Manrique, Rodrigo Ponce de
Leon and Captain Miranda. On the march 'certain gentle-
men of account' had died. They were: Don Garcia de
Avila, Don Gaspar de Avila, Don Christobal Maldonado,
Don Diego de Guzman and Hernando Canaveral.

The English, whose espionage system was excellent,
had by this time learned that Maurice Fitzmaurice, son of
the fighting leader of Desmond, was on board one of the
Armada ships. They had not, however, learned of his
death at sea at the time Don Alonso de Luzon's interrogation took place. Don Alonso was asked about the
number of Irishmen on board the fleet and he answered:
'I know not the names of those of this country's birth that
were in Spain when I came from thence, but I did see a
tall young gentleman with a red beard and a sanguine
complexion of whose name I know not. This young
gentleman came forth with the Armada, but in what ship
I know not.'

After many weeks of negotiation, Don Alonso and his
companions were ransomed, sent to London from where
they were presumably allowed to return to Spain.
O'Donnell, Earl of Tyrconnell, returned to his home and
not long afterwards retired to a cloister to repent, perhaps,
for the passivity which led to the murder of hundreds of
the men of Spain.

CHAPTER FOURTEEN

DEATH AT THE BLASKETS

WHILE MEN were being drowned or slain on the coasts of Galway, Clare, Mayo, Sligo and Donegal, Juan Martinez de Recalde, Knight of Santiago, and a seafarer who knew more about the dangers of the Irish coast than any of the other commanders of the Armada squadrons, was far out in the Atlantic. There had never been a likelihood that with Juan Martinez de Recalde on board, his ship would have been trapped by the great bulge of County Mayo—as were so many other captains.

From the north-west his galleon, *San Juan de Portugal,* approached. Wan and weak in his illness, the old seadog who had been given command of the Biscayan squadron came on deck on the morning of September 5 when a shout from the look-out high in the rigging called out a landfall. The cries of the Spaniards who had sufficient strength to shout were heard in a second ship, also named *San Juan,* but in this case she was *San Juan de Bautista*— a vessel of the squadron of Castile, and now keeping company with Juan de Recalde.

The galleon in which de Recalde sailed was big—1,150 tons and she carried 500 men. Roped to her decks behind the shuttered gun-ports were twenty heavy cannon, among them some of the most powerful guns in the entire Spanish fleet. The second *San Juan* was smaller, of 750 tons burthen and she had on board 243 men. Among that number was Marcos de Aramburu, Comptroller and Paymaster of the galleons of Castile, who left an account in the archives of Spain of the adventures and hardships he experienced on the coast of Ireland. With these two vessels sailed a third ship—undoubtedly the Scottish fishing-smack which Juan de Recalde had made a prize of war and the crew of which he had taken on board his galleon. The experienced seaman knew that there would be close inshore work for a vessel of shallow draught to do, and, besides, the nets on the fishing-smack would catch fish for the starving crews of the Spanish ships. The landfall was the great towering bulk of Mount Brandon, the huge mass of mountain which dominates Dingle Bay. The mountain, eight miles long from Brandon Point to the pass above Kilmalkedar, and five miles broad, deeply scored on the eastern side into spurs and valleys, is usually covered in cloud in autumn. When the look-out saw the dim outline of its bulk on the horizon the high winds would have stripped the mountain of its cloudy veil. As they sailed closer they saw the Blasket Islands, in the mouth of Dingle Bay, off the rugged coast of Kerry.

For more than sixteen years Juan Martinez de Recalde had been commanding Spanish fleets. In that time he had become a skilled tactician in sea-battles, a superb navigator within the limits of the knowledge and equipment of his day, and in seamanship he had acquired a hard-won expertise. As a commander of battle-fleets he had won for his King possession of the Azores, and his knowledge of the oceans had been broadened by several trips with the Indian Guard. Between times, he was given the post of Superintendent of the Royal Dockyards, so that there was little about sailing, navigation, fighting and the construction and repair of ships which Juan de Recalde did not know.

This native of Bilbao was, perhaps, the most famous Spanish seaman after Santa Cruz, and in the fighting in the Channel his ship shared with Don Alonso de Leyva's *La Rata Santa Maria Encoronada* the posts of greatest danger and responsibility. Never in the long drawn-out battle could the Duke of Medina Sidonia have had reason to blame his Vice-Admiral who sailed in *San Juan de Portugal*. When off the Eddystone, the English ships had assailed the Biscayan squadron which acted as rearguard it was Juan de Recalde and his veteran crew who had beaten off Drake in the *Revenge*, Hawkins in the *Victory* and Frobisher in the *Triumph* by a classic example of ship-handling. In that engagement twenty men on the *San Juan de Portugal* were killed, two round-shot from English culverins had damaged her mainmast, and rigging and stays had been shot away. In his ship's gallant fight against the most experienced of the English seamen, Juan de Recalde had been aided by the captain of the *Gran Grin,* the ship which was to find her last resting place at the mouth of Clew Bay in County Mayo. From Portland Bill to Calais Roads, de Recalde's galleon was in the thick of the fighting—trading powerful broadsides with the biggest of the English warships.

Marcos de Aramburu sailed in a ship which had also been severely damaged in the engagements in the Channel, but unlike many other vessels she had not lost all her cables and anchors off Calais when escaping from the fire-ships. The account which de Aramburu wrote would never have been written if his ship had not followed the vessel of Juan Martinez de Recalde.

On September 11, de Aramburu's ship had been floundering off the coast with no one on board quite certain of their position. They came close enough to sight two islands—probably Teraght and Tooskert—and as fast as their weakened canvas would permit they had tacked out to sea. With the wind south-south-west, they held to a westerly course as far as they were able to do so. Their anxiety to put as many leagues as possible between them and that part of the Irish coast is understandable. From the direction from which they approached they would have seen a fearful vista of white-topped waves thundering over rocks and sunken reefs.

At four o'clock in the afternoon the wind began to freshen and the sea began to get up. Soon they were taking green water. Below deck, scores of men were so crushed into small spaces that only the most restricted movement

was possible. Among them were men whose pallor was
the pallor of death, men who retched in gasping and ever-
weakening convulsions. When at last these men were still
and silent and when their mouths fell agape, the Spaniards
slid their dead into the sea. It happened every day, now
it was happening almost every hour. These men were
desperate. They had to reach land. They had to have
fresh water and food. The alternative to a death from
drowning in shipwreck was slow death from starvation,
thirst or disease.

By five o'clock the *San Juan Bautista* began to shudder
as the wind sprang at her from the south. 'It blew,' wrote
de Aramburu, 'with such force that at night there was a
most violent storm with a very wild sea and great darkness
on account of the clouds.'

Through the spume and the horizontal sheets of rain
the men on deck saw a ship near them in an equally
perilous plight. This vessel was the *Trinidad,* an 800-ton
merchant-ship converted to war purposes with twenty-four
guns and a complement of 302 men. The *Trinidad* kept
station with de Aramburu's vessel for some time until she
disappeared from their ken an hour before dawn. She
was never seen again. There is a record by Geoffrey
Fenton, Secretary to the Council in Dublin, that a Spanish
ship with 300 men on board was 'lost on the coast of
Desmond', but apart from this brief statement there is
no other confirmation. In Elizabethan Ireland a reference
to 'Desmond' meant that part of County Kerry south of
Dingle Bay. In tradition the wreck of a Spanish ship is
remembered near Valentia Island, and tradition also
claims the Maharees Sound and Muclachmor Rock
as locations of Armada wrecks. At any of these places
the ill-fated *Trinidad* may have foundered.

When dawn came the look-outs on *San Juan Bautista*
scanned the horizon for sight of mast-tips, but nothing
interrupted the storm-hazed circle around them. With
the morning came a rapid swing of the wind to north-west

and the sea began to calm. South-east sailed the *San Juan Bautista*. September 14 saw her on the same course and with the same wind. At noon de Aramburu saw to leeward a big ship with a smaller vessel astern. They were far off, but gradually the *San Juan Bautista* worked down towards them. At nightfall a mile separated them, but when complete darkness set in, the ships lost contact. On the *San Juan Bautista* lanterns were kept burning all night on forepeak and poop.

'On September 15,' wrote de Aramburu, 'we were running south with the wind west when two hours before daybreak we saw a vessel to the windward of us, showing us light and going north, and another to leeward which had no lantern burning. We thought they were the same as those of the previous evening, and that they were trying to get away from the land of which we, too, were in dread. Until day broke we kept on the course we were going. When light came we saw ahead of us two large islands, and to port in the east, the mainland, and as we could not weather it we turned to north-north-west.'

It was another example of the complexities of the Irish coast with which all the Spanish ships were confronted as they sought to find a sheltered bay on this tortuous shoreline.

Fortune smiled on de Aramburu as they again sighted the two vessels that had been their companions in distress during the night. They recognised the flagship of Juan Martinez de Recalde and close to her sailed a ship which de Aramburu described as a tender. 'We turned towards them,' he recorded, 'in our desperation with the wind athwart, and we ignorant of the coast and of any remedy.' De Aramburu did not know it at the time, but the keen-eyed look-outs who had sighted the lantern on the poop of de Recalde's galleon had saved the lives of all who sailed in the *San Juan Bautista*. Alone they could never have found the anchorage to which de Recalde had guided them. The pilot of the *San Juan Bautista* had no accurate charts.

Without them the approach to the Blaskets would be enough to try the nerves of the bravest.

The Great Blasket Island—a ridge four miles long, half-a-mile wide and nearly 600 feet high along its knife-like backbone—would frighten any sailor. The other islands which surround it are guarded by steep cliffs. Even in a summer swell the Atlantic combers break heavily on the sunken reefs and leap up against the sheer black walls of the island bastions. It is a place that calls for wariness and a lifetime of knowledge of reefs, tides and currents. The Great Blasket, Inishtooskert and Inish-vickillane were the islands which sheltered the famished, thirst-mad and exhausted Spaniards.

On board the *San Juan Bautista* there was astonishment as they watched Juan Martinez de Recalde's great galleon, the *San Juan de Portugal,* approach this cluster of islands and its concealed dangers in an angry confusion of rocks and seething sea. To them it seemed that in the great rollers whose heads curved over in creaming foam the galleon would be smashed against the sinister black shape of Carraig Fhada which appeared and disappeared under successive surges of the waves. Destruction must surely await this proud ship of the Armada.

The man who brought the *San Juan de Portugal* to her anchorage at the Blaskets showed consummate skill in his seamanship. How he dared the passage of the reefs is explained by de Aramburu: 'He kept approaching the land and ran into the port of Vicey through an entrance between low rocks and about as wide as the length of a ship, and then he anchored.' The reference to 'the port of Vicey' is undoubtedly to the island of Inishvickillane. Juan de Recalde passed to the westward of Inishtooskert, and, turning east, ran before the wind close to the hazard of Carraig Fhada (The Long Rock), and so reached his anchorage which had a sandy bottom. This narrow passage was selected, perhaps, in preference to the wider one between Beginish and the mainland, because, with a

westerly wind, the galleon might have failed to luff up
to the anchorage. Failure would have meant destruction
at the foot of the cliffs at Dunquin or on the promontory
of Dun Mhor. In selecting his anchorage, de Recalde
made certain that the only wind which would make it
unsafe would be a fair wind for Spain.

In all this there is the question: How did the *San Juan
de Portugal* sail so confidently through such a hazardous
passage. Once before de Recalde had been off the Kerry
coast to land the small expeditionary force from Spain
which was massacred after the surrender of Dun an Oir.
But that voyage could scarcely have provided him with
the intimate knowledge which would enable him to sail
his vessel through a passage that was only a ship's length
in width in the island-cluster of the Blaskets. He had
with him the Scottish crew who had been taken from the
fishing-smack. It is possible that these Scotsmen knew
the dangerous entrance to the shelter of the islands and
brought the galleon to the place with the sandy bottom
where the anchors could be let go.

Yet there are better and safer anchorages along that
section of the coast which they would have known if it
had been their custom to fish in those waters. In the
Dingle peninsula there is a traditional belief that it was
a sailor from Dingle who steered the galleon past Carraig
Fhada—and tradition more often than not speaks with
truth.

The balance of probabilities leans towards the theory
that an Irishman did the pilotage. The Scots may have
known safer anchorages or harbours, but an Irishman
would know that the ships which anchored in the shelter
of the Blaskets would be remote from English interference
while provisions were obtained ashore and repairs were
made to the galleon on which he sailed. This expectation,
however, was not completely fulfilled.

The *San Juan Bautista* followed in the wake of the
San Juan de Portugal into the sound and the two big ships

were later joined by the small fishing vessel. At once
parties in small boats were sent ashore. They succeeded
in obtaining water and provisions—a fact which the
Queen's representatives did not unduly emphasise in
making their reports of subsequent events. The first of
these reports went from Dominick Ryesse (or Rice) to
Lord Deputy Fitzwilliam in Dublin: 'There arrived in the
Sound of Blasgay two ships and a frigate, and afore their
arriving they did send a boat ashore and landed three of
their men, and the boat—by the foul weather—was also
afterwards set ashore with five other men.'

These eight men were captured, and Dominick Rice
continued: 'Among them was a Scotsman who said he was
captured at sea, and he also saith that in the two ships
and frigate there were 1,000 men, and the most part of
them are sick, destitute of victual and in great extremity
from want of knowledge.'

On the Spanish side, de Aramburu wrote: 'Juan Martinez
de Recalde gave us two cables and an anchor, for we had
nothing but the cable which was down, and I gave him
an anchor of 30 cwt., which was of no use to us, and of
which he stood in the greatest need.' No chances were
taken when the next searchers for food and water were
sent ashore. In the long-boat from the Armada galleon
went a strong force of arquebusiers who landed far away
from a group of soldiers who served Queen Elizabeth and
who waved a white flag on which there was a red
cross.

'For three days,' recorded de Aramburu, 'we remained
at the same port without being able to get out. Juan
Martinez went on taking water, and I, having no long-
boat nor other boat, could do little, and that with much
labour.'

While the Spanish vessels at the Blaskets were being
made ready for the resumption of their voyage, a small
ship of the Armada was threshing around in the vastness
of the Atlantic. The Spaniards would have classed her as

a *zabra*—a sloop of many uses, a despatch boat, a ship of light draught. She may have been the *Nuestra Senora del Socorro*, of 75 tons. In desperate straits the commander of this little ship sailed south-east until he sighted the Kerry coast. Tradition tells that he anchored at Fenit. Without a small-boat, three of the crew volunteered to swim ashore to parley with those whom they might encounter and to seek water and provisions.

The parley with the officers of the Queen resulted in terms which have, so far, never been revealed. The effect was that the entire company, 'all of Castile and Biscay', surrendered themselves and their vessel. This haggard and sea-weary group were then marched off to confront Lady Margaret Denny, wife of Sir Edward Denny, in what was then the village of Tralee. They passed under the portcullis of the castle and entered the great hall where flares cast eerie shadows on flagged floor and rough-plastered walls. When the castaways were brought before her, Lady Denny gave a dreadful order. Without pity she said: 'Let all of them hang—there is no prison here that is big enough or safe enough to keep them.'

Three of the captives pleaded that they had friends in Waterford who would aid them in arranging ransom. The plea went unheeded. It might have influenced this pitiless woman if her captives had given the names of those in Waterford who would be prepared to negotiate a ransom, but this the prisoners refused to do. On the following day a gibbet was erected at the Market Cross in Tralee and all 24 Spaniards were hanged in barbaric fashion— by slow strangulation. The next day, Sir Edward Denny rode back to Tralee from Dublin where he had attended a meeting of the Council—to hear that great ships of the Armada had anchored at the Blaskets. The news brought fear to the heart of Sir Edward Denny. For him the landing of a Spanish force could bring a terrible retribution.

CHAPTER FIFTEEN

GRAVE OF THE PRINCE

SIR EDWARD DENNY was a typical Englishman in the Ireland of the days of Queen Elizabeth the First. There were many hundreds like him—younger sons of new-rich English families who sought land and wealth in Ireland. Their presence serves to explain the cruel and harsh treatment which was accorded to thousands who sailed with the Spanish Armada when they came ashore in Ireland. The appetite of the Denny family had been whetted for easily acquired wealth in England where Sir Anthony Denny, father of Sir Edward, at the dissolution of the monasteries, had been awarded the Priory at Hertford, a great part of Waltham Abbey, in Essex, and most of the enormously wealthy abbatial estates of St. Albans, with eleven extra parishes thrown in for good measure.

There was nothing unusual in the coming of Edward Denny to a country which he described in a letter to his cousin, Francis Walsingham, as 'more suited to mastiffs than gentlemen'. He came to Ireland on what was virtually the equivalent of a modern assisted-passage scheme. Those who set out from England were called Undertakers. If they so desired, they could become settlers in the Geraldine lands which were portioned out in 12,000, 8,000, 6,000 and 4,000 acres.

Every Undertaker bound himself to 'plant' a certain number of English families on this land. Those who took over 12,000 acres, for example, would engage to bring over eighty English families, to retain for his own family 1,500 acres, and to give the tenancy of 400 acres to a chief farmer and to the remainder lesser acreages which were carefully set out in the agreement.

The plan was taken up with enthusiasm by hundreds

of Englishmen on whose behalf it was calculated that a sum of £278 would be sufficient for wages, food, stock and seed for the first year of occupation. Sir Edward Denny took a modest 6,000 acres and was given the castle at Tralee for an even more modest one hundred pounds.

Those who ruled England hoped that the Irish colony would absorb some of the thousands of peasants who were roaming the English countryside workless and landless —a danger and a serious social problem. There had been great changes in the English land system in the sixteenth century as lands were enclosed and the conversion of arable land to pasture lessened the demand for labour. But the plan did not work. The Undertakers failed to bring over English colonists. They took the easier course of sub-letting their lands to Irish tenants from whom they could obtain higher rents. Thus it came about that the diaspora of the Irish never took place. The system merely introduced foreign landlords instead of the expected English population.

Sir Edward Denny was one of those who helped at the ghastly massacre at Dun an Oir in 1580, when, after the surrender of the mixed Spanish and Italian force, hundreds of headless bodies were thrown on to the sand at the shoreline. For his 'gallantry' he was knighted, and shortly afterwards he brought his bride, Margaret Edgecombe, maid of honour to the Queen, to his castle at Tralee. His method of ensuring peace in his domain was the use of terror—a follower of O'Sullivan Mor had his ears cut off for saying that he knew no ruler but his own chieftain. It was to this man that James Trant, from Dingle, penned this report: 'Three great ships, one of 900 tons, ride at anchor betwixt Ferriter's main island and the shore. The Prince of Ascoli, base son to the King of Spain, is drowned with 500 tall men in the ship named *Santa Maria de la Rosa*.'

Sir Edward at once set out for the Dingle peninsula to join the force of Sir Thomas Norris, Vice-President of the Council of Munster, who had reported: 'I am hastening to the Blasgays with 200 foot and fifty horse.'

The English force rode and marched through a storm which sent turbulent waves against the islands of the Blaskets where the *San Juan de Portugal*, the *San Juan Bautista* and the little fishing vessel strained at their anchors as the fury of wind and sea mounted with each hour.

'The wind began to blow from the west with terrible violence,' wrote Marcos de Aramburu. 'Then the ship of Juan Martinez de Recalde drifted down on us. We dropped anchor with another cable, and, having smashed our lantern and the tackle on our mizzenmast, we brought the ship to.'

When this storm died down, the galleon *Santa Maria de la Rosa*, vice-flagship of the Squadron of Guipuzcoa, and commanded by Martin de Villafranca, entered between the knife-edged rocks which guarded the anchorage. Her pilot, not knowing the narrow entrance which de Recalde had used, came in by another entrance as de Aramburu explains, 'nearer the land towards the north-west'.

It became quickly apparent to de Recalde and de Aramburu that something was seriously amiss with the *Santa Maria de la Rosa*. In the full light of mid-day they saw her enter. All her sails, with the exception of foresail, were torn to ribbons. In a distress-signal a gun boomed from her deck as her commander sighted the other ships, then another gun-shot thudded over the water as she dropped a single anchor—all that she had left. The tide, which was coming in from the south-east, beat against her stern, but still the lone anchor held.

The anchor held until two o'clock and at that time, de Aramburu recorded: 'When the tide began to ebb the *Santa Maria de la Rosa* began to drift about two splices of cable from us, and we with her. In an instant we saw that she was going to the bottom while many men on deck tried to hoist the foresail. At once she went down with the whole crew—not a soul escaping—a most extraordinary and terrible occurrence. We were drifting down upon her and to our perdition. It pleased our Lord that for that passage, and in case of such a necessity, we had put a new stock to an anchor which Juan Martinez de Recalde had given us and which had only half a stock. We dropped this anchor and our head came around. Then we hauled in our first anchor and found how narrow had been our escape for half the shank was broken off and the cable had been chafed by the rocks over which we were lying.'

Marcos de Aramburu went back to Spain in the belief that all of the 297 men who sailed in the 900-ton *Santa Maria de la Rosa* had been drowned. There was one survivor—a young man named Antonia de Monana.

It is interesting to speculate on the various points at which this great ship may have perished. Those ships which first entered the sound chose their anchorages wisely—between Beginish and the Great Blasket, all islands once in Desmond possession, but which had been given to the famous Norman-Irish family of the Ferriters. It is probable that in the gale they dragged their anchors in an easterly direction and were finally anchored on rocks about the ten-fathom line. The *Santa Maria de la Rosa,* which had been anchored near them, must have been blown halfway across the sound. Some experts believe that she sank near Stromboli rock. This rock, lying three fathoms beneath the surface of the sea today, may have been above water when the ships of the Armada sought shelter in the Blasket Sound. Almost a hundred years ago a British warship ran aground on the rock and in doing so broke off a large section. The name of the warship was *Stromboli* —hence the name of the rock as marked on modern charts.

Four hours after the waters of the sound had closed over the *Santa Maria de la Rosa* the converted merchantman, *San Juan de Ragusa,* a vessel of 650 tons, a crew of 285, and commanded by Fernando Horra, arrived. Then there sailed in another ship—nameless in the archives— commanded by Miguel de Aranivar.

The *San Juan de Ragusa* had been severely damaged

since she had parted with the fleet off the Orkneys. Her
mainmast had been toppled and at the moment in which
she entered the sound her foresail was blown to shreds.
'It was impossible to communicate with her or to help
her,' commented de Aramburu, 'but on the following day
Fernando Horra lowered his long-boat and made known
his distressed condition. His vessel was sinking and Juan
Martinez de Recalde decided that I should take the whole
company commanded by Gonzalo Melendez and dis-
tribute that commanded by Diego Bazan on the tender.
I urged Juan Martinez to give me permission to leave,
putting before him my distressed condition, and, being
without a boat, I could not supply myself with water while
bread and other stores were being used up. I urged him
to set fire to the sinking ship and to allow me to start.
But he wished me to remove the guns from Fernando
Horra's vessel and to make a special effort to do so, which
was impossible. So in the presence of all the commanders
he gave me leave to go.'

Quite close to Dunquin a finger of concrete juts out
from the cliffs. Near this pier there is a sheltering curve
of rock, and where this reef narrows to needle sharpness
it is called Dunbinna. Since 1588, fathers have been telling
their sons that Dunbinna is the point at which a ship of
the Armada sank. But was this where the *Santa Maria
de la Rosa* sank to the bottom or is it the place where the
San Juan de Ragusa rests? No one knows with certainty.

While the Spanish ships lay in the sound the forces of
Queen Elizabeth were assembling at Dingle to meet the
invasion of Spaniards which they expected to take place
at any moment. The eight men who formed the Spanish
reconnaissance party which de Recalde had sent ashore,
all of whom had been captured, were interrogated inten-
sively. One of them, Emmanuel Fremoso, a Portuguese,
told his interrogator: 'There was in de Recalde's ship
only 25 pipes of wine, very little bread and no water, but
what they had brought out of Spain and it stinketh

marvellously. Their flesh meat they cannot eat, and their thirst is great. The main mast of the Admiral's ship is so weakened by shot that they dare not bear the sails they might to take them to Spain. The best men in the ship are scarcely able to stand and they do lie down and die daily.'

From Emmanuel Francisco, another Portuguese, this information was extracted: 'The best that be in the Admiral's ship are so weak that if they tarry where they are for any time they will all perish.'

All this information was comforting to the men who upheld the rule of Queen Elizabeth. If the Spaniards were so weakened there would be little to fear.

The English, among them Sir Edward Denny who had by this time reached Dingle, had another prisoner whose name was Antonia de Monana—sole survivor of the sinking of the *Santa Maria de la Rosa*. He had floated ashore on a plank and was found unconscious and almost lifeless on the shore when the tide had receded. When he had recovered consciousness he was brought to Dingle and there questioned by an interpreter named David Gwynn in the presence of James Trant.

Among the yellow-aged documents in the archives of England there still exists a page of closely-written handwriting which gives one of the most unusual sidelights of the Armada. It is the report of the interrogation of Antonia de Monana. He was an Italian, and he may have been a young man of great astuteness. In his account he did not minimise the quantity of loot which could be obtained by those who knew the exact place where the *Santa Maria de la Rosa* had sunk. He may have reasoned that, as he was the only survivor, his life might be spared so that he could pinpoint the position of the wreck. Antonia de Monana also said he was the son of the ship's pilot and that his father had been killed by the sword of the captain just before the vessel sank. The captain had shouted 'traitor' before plunging his sword to the hilt in the body of his pilot, and moments later the vessel sank.

In this dramatic story the young man gained two advantages. As the son of the pilot he could be expected to know something about taking bearings, and the murder of his father—if this had ever occurred—would provide a strong reason for helping the English to recover Spanish treasure. Antonia listed the names of many Spanish grandees who had been on board, and he said that within a certain cabin there were 50,000 ducats, an equal amount in silver, and great quantities of gold and silver plate. The ship, he declared, carried fifty guns, all cannon of the field, of which 25 were of brass. For good measure, perhaps, he threw in the information that the *Maria de la Rosa* carried fifty tons of wine in her aft-hold.

Then he told his questioner that the natural son of the King of Spain—the Prince of Ascoli—had been on board. He described the Prince as 'a slender man of about 28 years of age, with a high forehead, of reasonable stature, with brown hair stroked upwards, with very little beard, and palefaced with some little red in his cheeks.' Then he went on to describe what the Prince had worn just before the shipwreck . . . . 'a suit of white satin, a doublet and breeches cut after the Spanish mode, and with russet silk stockings.'

This was not true. The Prince of Ascoli had set sail with the Armada. But when the fleet lay off the French coast he was charged with the duty of conveying instructions from ship to ship. He did this duty and then landed at Dunkirk. That ended his connection with the great enterprise of invasion. The story that the Prince had been drowned in the Blasket Sound spread all over Ireland and was quickly sent to London in many messages which reached Walsingham and Burghley. When hundreds of bodies were washed ashore on the Kerry mainland, they were buried. Near the schoolhouse at Dunquin there is a spot which has been known for centuries as Uaig Mhic

Ri na Spainne—The Grave of the Son of the King of Spain. The grave may contain the bones of many high-born Spaniards, but it is certainly not the resting place of King Philip's natural son.

It is not improbable that the story attributed to Antonia de Monana is complete fiction—imaginatively created by the man who conducted his interrogation. David Gwynn was a liar, a thief, a scoundrel—but of these qualities in his character his English employers were unaware until a much later date. How this glib Welshman came to be at Dingle to conduct the interrogation of the Spanish castaways is an adventure story in itself. He claimed that in a sea-fight some years before the Armada sailed he had been captured by the crew of a Spanish ship. For more than a year he was kept at the oar of a galley, and it was on board this vessel that he had sailed with the Armada. The storm which had overtaken the Armada off Corunna had driven the galley, *Diana*, on which he was one of the slave-oarsmen, towards Bayonne.

David Gwynn told a heroic tale of how he had freed his fellow-slaves, killed almost single-handed her entire Spanish crew, had then captured three other galleys of the Armada and brought them all to a French port. It never happened, but the truth took a long time to overtake this colourful yarn. After his return to England he was rushed to Ireland as interpreter-interrogator of the Spanish captives. Having confirmed that Antonia de Monana was the sole survivor of the *Santa Maria de la Rosa*, Gwynn may have been tempted to give his employers full value for their money in the relatively safe knowledge that the story could not be refuted. Within a few days it stood less chance of refutation—for all those who had fallen into the hands of Sir Edward Denny at Dingle, including Antonia de Monana, were executed.

They died on the day that Marcos de Aramburu in the *San Juan Bautista* took advantage of an ebb tide and tried to get out of the sound through the main southern entrance.

He failed in this, and with the flood-tide he had to turn to try the passage to north-west among the reefs.

'On the morning of September 23,' he wrote, 'we set out with a light easterly wind, and on leaving the port of Vicey at a distance of two cables the wind dropped while the current was carrying us to an island, so that we were near being lost. The wind got up again, and we went out with top-gallant sails set as far as the reefs which lie to the north, and there the wind fell calm again while the tide was drifting us on to the land to the north between four islands and the reefs. We anchored before nightfall with one spring, as we had no more, and an hour after darkness came the wind began to blow from the south-east. The ship began to drift on to the islands which are so rocky that no one coming on to them could be saved. We brought the ship round with the spring, and, weighing anchor, set sail—commending ourselves to Our Lord, not knowing whether there was any way out. A desperate venture was this in a dark and cloudy night. We tried to get to windward of the reefs, but the current would not allow us, rather was it carrying us to destruction. We turned and tried by an opening between the islands. The wind was freshening still more, and there was a sea running with heavy clouds and violent showers. It pleased Our Lady, to whom we commended ourselves, that we should get out, and we sailed all that night to the west, so that by morning we were eight leagues from the land.'

The crowded company on the *San Juan Bautista* must have sighed with relief at that point in their adventures, but more trials were in store for them. On the following day, three hours after daybreak, a violent storm burst upon them. Once more clouds of tremendous size scudded across the Atlantic. Once more rain hissed down until the sea was a turmoil of white.

This storm, although of great strength, did not last long. After three hours a rift came in the dark sky to the west. The sea became less angry and the rain ceased. The ship lay-to. Then the wind veered to the west. This seemed to be the prelude of doom for the *San Juan Bautista* and for all who sailed in her. Stripped of all sail, the battered vessel laboured in the curving canyons of the foam-flecked waves as the wind forced her nearer and nearer to land. Again they were reprieved. The wind abated in the evening and the crew were able to haul at the sails once more. Darkness came and with it a moderate wind. The ship sailed slowly over the ever-restless sea. When dawn broke they found themselves at the opening to the Blasket Sound from which they had made their escape.

These sorely tried men could have been pardoned if they thought themselves forsaken by God. Grimly they looked at the land from which, it seemed, they could never escape. They could scarcely believe their good fortune when gently at first, then with increasing strength, a wind blew from the south-east and before its invisible pressure the ship tacked seawards. All that day of September 25 and all that night they sailed until they judged their distance from the coast at ten leagues.

But de Aramburu's troubles were not ended. On September 28 the wind shifted suddenly to south and south-south-west and the helmsman was ordered to change course. At midnight the *San Juan Bautista* was buffeted by another gale. Now the wind had veered north-west and the foresail was blown to shreds. Down came the main top-sail, but in the howling storm the sailors could not furl it. The canvas flapped and tugged, threatening to capsize the ship. Below deck the heavy cannon had been stored atop the gravel and sand ballast. These weighty brass and cast-iron guns shifted to port, and when the vessel heeled over she was struck by three waves of extra-ordinary height in the waist. Those Spaniards were great seamen. In these dreadful conditions they got up a studding-sail on the fore-tackle and with this they got the ship under control. The *San Juan Bautista* sailed on towards Spain.

Three days after the departure of the *San Juan Bautista*
the ships under the command of Juan Martinez de Recalde
set sail from the Blaskets. All of them reached Spanish
ports, but Juan Martinez, that courageous old sailor,
did not live long after his return. His illness had been too
severe and within a month he was dead.

The centuries rolled on and the sea still rushed through
the Blaskets. Then—about eighty years ago—a fisherman
dragged up from the seabed a small brass cannon. On
this gun was a coat of arms—an uprooted tree with a
band across it. That was all that the sea gave up of those
ships which sank on the Kerry coast.

The village of Tralee grew into a town and the castle
of Sir Edward Denny became a ruin. The great hall stood
roofless—the hall in which Lady Denny had pronounced
her death sentence. And as the years passed, the stones
of the castle were pulled down to make a new roadway.
That roadway became a street in Tralee and its name today
is Denny Street.

CHAPTER SIXTEEN

THE AFTERMATH

THE MAIN PART of the Spanish fleet had sailed far out of
sight of the Irish coast. Obediently following the instructions of the Duke of Medina Sidonia, the sixty ships kept
station on his flagship, the *San Martin,* and all of them
safely rounded Cape Clear. All except a few. One of these
was the *Gran Grifon,* a big store-ship which had become
separated from the main group. She had been so severely
damaged that her survival depended on a day-and-night
operation of the pumps. For many days she was blown
hither and thither until she reached a point far west of
Galway Bay. From there she was blown back upon her

course until her master sighted the Outer Hebrides. In pitch darkness the *Gran Grifon* ran aground on Fair Island. The crew were able to get to shore and from there they were able to reach the Scottish mainland. Another of the Spanish galleons sank in Tobermory Bay.

As the fleet reached the lower latitudes the gales ceased. They sailed on outside Scilly and into the Bay of Biscay. The Duke of Medina Sidonia sighted Corunna, but the crew of the *San Martin* were so weakened that they could not work their ship into the harbour. Distress signals were flown, but no vessel put out to aid them and the flagship of the Armada dropped to leeward to Bilbao. The ship commanded by Oquendo reached Santander.

Day by day the other ships made their landfall at one or other of the Biscay ports. The suffering of the crews did not end there. Hospital beds were few and there was no organisation to provide them with food. Many hundreds were left on board to die because those on land feared that a plague had struck the ships. Within a few days Juan Martinez de Recalde and Oquendo were dead. The Duke who led them was so ill that a week passed before he could be removed on a litter to his home at San Lucar.

All this was reported back to Ireland through the agency of a merchant named William Herbert. He returned from Spain to describe the wailing of the people, the hanging of the bakers who had sailed with the fleet, and the ban which King Philip had imposed on the Duke of Medina Sidonia. The King, according to William Herbert, had forbidden the Duke to approach within seven leagues of his court.

The tales of this traveller were untrue. In Spain there was grief, but the defeat of the King's invasion purpose was accepted. None of those who returned was made to suffer for lack of success, and, in fact, the Duke of Medina Sidonia continued to serve the monarch as Governor of Cadiz.

William Herbert added another tit-bit of news to his

report when he said that 'in the holy house of Lisbon they did in great fury burn their holy woman'. This was a reference to the widely-held belief that a nun in a Lisbon convent had assured the King of Spain the Armada would be successful in the invasion of England—of this she had been told in a vision. The story was believed in England and in Ireland although it was completely unfounded in fact.

More accurate was the account brought back by Edward Walsh to Waterford. He said that the Duke of Medina Sidonia had stayed on board the *San Martin* for six days and had then been carried ashore, followed by fifty gentlemen in mourning. 'And,' he added, 'the like lamentation was never heard in any country.'

And so the tragic tale of the Armada came to a close. The Atlantic still sweeps against the western coast of Ireland, stirring in its depths some rotted or corroded remnant of this proud fleet. Men still point to a headland or bay and say: 'A Spanish ship was wrecked there long, long ago.'

A pitiful postscript to this fantastic enterprise of King Philip of Spain was written by Lord Deputy Fitzwilliam, and read with satisfaction in London: 'There remains of the Armada in Ireland about 100 or thereabouts, being both miserable in body and apparel, and few or none of them Spaniards.' A second postscript was written by envoys of the Spanish King who came to Ireland in 1596 to make inquiry for survivors. They found only eight.

THE END